Ch. W. Rosenfeld

Torat ha-adam

The Teachings of Humanity

Ch. W. Rosenfeld

Torat ha-adam
The Teachings of Humanity

ISBN/EAN: 9783337250027

Printed in Europe, USA, Canada, Australia, Japan

Cover: Foto ©Lupo / pixelio.de

More available books at **www.hansebooks.com**

THE
Teachings ✦ of ✦ Humanity

A TREATISE

throwing some light on certain movemements of the day

BY CH. W. ROSENFELD.

Translated from Hebrew by M. M.

LONDON.

1890.

PREFACE.

Our Sages say: "Blessed be the generation, whose great men listen carefully to what others less important than themselves have to say". Again the say: "Just as a small burning candle can light a big fire so can sometimes an ordinary man enlighten those who have reached already to fame". I do not pretend to place myself amongst the great or even the learned but nevertheless, I feel, I can be useful by communicating my experience to my fellow-men.

Having carefully studied and examined the character of different shades and classes of our fellow-men, I feel that many will agree with my ideas and conclusions, and those I intend to awaken and induce to use their best efforts and endeavour to ameliorate the state of our poor brethren and to implant into their hearts the love to each other. I also wish to show to the Antisemites especially, that our Law is strictly based on principles of morals and humanity pointing and leading to the way on which all can be united. I hear a question: "How can a perfect union practically be brought about?" The never forgotten Maimonides (Rambam) says: "If there were no fools and madmen the world could not exist". Curious as these words seem, they prove perfectly true after a careful examination. Though logically speaking two contrary reactions can never act simultaneously, yet we find for instance that the mutual reactions existing between heaven and earth are quite opposed to each other and that these very reactions the power of repelling on one hand that of attraction on the other make both of them keep in firm state of constant and inevitable dependence of each other. Physical theory shows that every thing we see and observe is composed of little parts (atoms) which equally attract and repell each other and yet they exist and remain in connection with each other by the power of attraction. Such is the case also with the revolvings of the earth and heavenly bodies. We see also opposed extremes in nature as summer and winter, heat and cold, life and death all contributing and absolutely necesssary to the existence of the world and mankind. We find also proofs of it in Meteorology, Physics and Chemistry. Chlor and Natron for instance, each separately taken being a strong poison for itself, when united, produce salt, an article indispensable in human life We come to the same conclusion if we consider the positive and negative electricity and magnetism, two opposed extremes, and see that without these very two extremes electricity or magnetism and its principles would be impossible. We find it also to be so with art, trade and science. Every human being shows an inclination to another branch of art, science or trade, and whilst reaching a certain degree of perfection in this one special branch disregards the other branches, yet this is very good and practical since union of all branches has, does and will produce all articles we invent, and find in our every day's life. If people would only want clothing to cover their nakedness and to warm them, we could only employ one thousandth part of working hands actually engaged in supplying our wants. Only because every one likes and finds pleasure in one special fancy, colour shape or

make, disliking any other, we can give work to those
thousands who need it. True we must call those who fancy
certain shape and colour or fashion to some extent madmen,
but as we have shown such must exist in the world. These
fancies give pleasure the every class of poeple and contribute
a great deal to encourage them to life, on the other hand
they support all those who offer opportunity to enjoy them.
But in as much as these enjoyments give pleasure to
one part, they can sometime hurt others, nay they can, when
satisfying one's inclination, ruin another morally and materially, and such kind of enjoyment involves upon those who
indulge in it, not only a great moral responsibility, but make
them severely answerable by law, which says that every
pleasure must be indulged temperately without bringing
hurt to anyone and does not acknowledge the satisfaction
of one's inclination or desire as a legal and reasonable excuse.
The same we find with nationalism and patriotism.

To many great and reknown men of war who have
shown themselves brave on the field of battle, although great
harm has been done by this to many a family, depriving
them of their father and husband, monuments are erected to
commemorate this bravery, or better saying, this cruel act of
humanity. But since now this has also been looked to, and
when I arrived here, I heard that humanity has so far advanced that a Congress has lately assembled to see and choose
ways and means, that wars should not be undertaken, unless
those who undertake them are necessarily compelled to do
so in order as to defend themselves, we must be grateful to
these promoters of noble humanity. I am sure this will bring
much good to mankind, and although we may not be able to

reach such standard at once, we must go slowly and educate the world by degrees as we do with a little child, and the further we will go in this way, the more perfection the world will attain, and a time will thus come when people will despise such monuments, hitherto so greatly esteemed.

We must also necessarily understand that no idea can be called reasonable, because it has a great many followers. The wise and great Boerne being once asked: "What is sense"? said: "The folly of the great majority". Thus as every creed regards another as a folly, as one profanes the holy relics of another, a Jew kissing the Fringes or frontlets, — a Christian kissing and embracing a wooden or metal cross. — we would be wrong in justifying one or the other so doing. So we can see some laughing at a woman in fashionable dress, others ridiculing one dressed to the contrary. The europeans laugh at the sight of a nigger, and the niggers despise the Caucasian race. But this laughing, despising and ridiculing on one side, the honouring, esteeming and respecting on the other, would not suffice to justify either of them. And this is what the legend tells of the Millennium that Elijah will come not to cleanse or profane the human race but to attract the ideas repelled by the majority and to repell such opinions that a great many have accepted and adhere to, to propagate morals and humanity repelling disregard, hatred and enmity. To repell "humanity"as understood hitherto by the so called "nationalists"and to attract true humanity and real nationalism. For the real principles of true nationalism are only that every one should support his fellowman, as a father supports and maintains his family, risking his life for their happiness and this helps the existence of the world. But as every one could not possibly care for all the world at a time, it would be well that every one should have a certain circle, for the welfare of which he should work with all his best efforts, however not hurting or ruining another working in the same direction. But by all means, we must not understand that everyone should care for his fellowmen as he cares for his own natural family, since this would be against nature, as our Rabbis say: "He who spends shall never spend more than one fifth of his income. So is the creed founded only to the good of the human race, thus showing, that we must, however we esteem our own creed, never laugh or ridicule another, nor must we look upon other poeples religous actions critically or with disregard. For the chief principle is that every one shall try to improve his own actions showing due respect to his neighbour. We must leave to Providence to lead a man to repent the wrong he may do towards his Creator and to the judges on earth to make poeple do right to their fellowmen.

We thus come to the conclusion that however important the repelling power may influence the world, to make ideas as different as faces of human race; the chief power is the "attracting strength" This essay is therefore called "Teaching of humanity" for according to Rabbi Akiba the word "האדם" means all mankind, signifying thus upon the neccessity of humanity in life. For if "Man has been created in the image of God", whoever has this image must be righteous and truthful, must be a man in the full sense of the word.

LONDON, NOVEMBER 13th, 1890.

The Author.

PREFACE

This work has been published as a humble thank offering to her most Gracious Majesty the Queen and Royal Family and to her Majesty's Ministers and also to the Nobility and Gentry of Great Britain for their humanity and advanced civilization and for their just and humane laws, also that there is no distinction between creeds, as I see one of my co-religionists elevated to the Peerage. This work was intended to be brought forth during the Mayoralty of Sir Henry Isaacs Bart. for the great pleasure I felt that the third time one of my co-religionists has been elevated to that great distinction of chief Magistrate of London. My work would have been forthcoming at the time, but as I had not sufficient command of the English language to undertake the work myself, I had to employ translators with whom I had great difficulty to convey my ideas, and there are many important items left out, owing to their inability to translate them, and then again I was not in such a condition financially to publish this book in such a manner as I intended.

I sincerely trust that this work will greatly interest you, as you will notice in page 17 it greatly alludes to the development of civilization and humanity of mankind. I wish to point out to those of my readers who wish to criticise this book that they will do so after looking over its contents thoroughly. This work strongly opposes Socialism, it is simply undertaken to propagate pure humanity amngst mankind.

July 15th 1891.   The Author.

N. B. The figures in the text indicate the notes which will be found at the end of the Book. A list of misprints is to be found on page 106 etc.

"The stranger that dwelleth with you, shall be unto you as one born among you and thou shalt love him as thyself" (*Leviticus XIX, 24*).

A stranger cannot but feel admiration and gratitude for the advanced principles of **humanity** among the English without regard to religious denomination, so strikingly displayed in the Election of a Jew for the dignity of Lord Mayor of London. Already 3000 years ago Moses based religion on this principle, as I hope to demonstrate in a special work. whilst I must be satisfied for the present with a short sketch. Indeed, he based religion on the love of God and love of Men, which two principles are identical; since the love of God can only be realised by benefitting humanity,(1) whereas true love of Man can only be attained through the love of God.(2) Even freethinkers, who, like Spinoza, invest nature with divine attributes, must admit that there is some hidden incomprehensible power at the bottom of it, and this idea underlies the prohibition of Moses to represent God by any image, for we can only know Him through His works. (3)

God's Work or nature offers an endless field for human investigation and exertions, and by thus raising himself to self-consciousness, man is enabled to appreciate the rights of others, which is implied in the commandment of Moses to love one's neighbour as oneself(4). The strictly orthodox R. Akiba called it the first principle of the Law, whilst his philosphical contemporary Ben Asai called it the Charter of Humanity(5). Hillel, too summarised the whole law to a convert in this single sentence: "Do not treat thy neighbour as you should not like to be treated yourself" The above mentioned R. Akiba placed the love of man on a level with the love of God, in whose image he was created, and this interpretation is applied by the commentators to all men without distinction of Race and creed (6).

Now, love of men finds its highest expression in the love of strangers, who are liable to excite ill-will of natives by their different manners and real or imaginary competition. That is why Moses has uttered not less than forty six injunctions to love the stranger, reminding them of their own condition of strangers in Egypt, and concluding with the formula: "I am the Lord", thus intimating the close connection between religion and humanity. I even consider the residence of the Jews in the land of Egypt as an act of Providence, having for its purpose the preparation of the Jews for such a humanitarian and hospitable religion.(7).

It is true, there are many who consider immigration as an evil, but they are mistaken, since notwithstanding its partial drawbacks and injuries to individuals, it is beneficial for the majority and even indirectly for the whole of the community. The prejudice against immigration is just so fallacious as that against machinery or cheap production, which are considered by some as a calamity, since there is no absolute and universal good, as there is no absolute evil. And these alternations of good and evil are necessary for the due apreciation of the first just as in the economy of nature the enjoyment of light is determined by the existence of darkness.

Hate against strangers is thus produced by unreasoning jealousy, which as the bible teaches us in the case of Cain and Abel was the first source of crime, though there were only two persons to divide the world. People do not consider that real happiness and abundance are only produced by mutual assistance and universal cooperation. Spain is a case in point, since through the Expulsion of the Jews it gained no advantages, but, on the contrary, is much inferior to countries in which there is a Jewish population.

The Jewish Law did not require a stranger to become a convert to Judaism, but merely imposed on him the essential claims of justice and morality as a condition of his addmission to the full rights of citizenship(8). He was merely required to relinquish the abominable practices of those peoples, of sacrificing their children and other barbarities(9). Our law is thus thoroughly based on principles of humanity, inspite of seeming exceptions, which I hope to explain in their true light on some future occassion. As Maimonides justly explains, sacrifices, which have no visible humanitarian purpose, were a necessary concession to the spirit of that age which was not yet sufficiently developed for a purely spiritual worship(10), and could only by these means be turned away from idolatry and pagan sacrifices; though later generations, attributed to them greater importance, either through ignorance or through the influence of a greedy clergy. But the prophets always protested against the sacrifices, and included no ceremonies whatever in their formulations of the Jewish creed, basing it exclusively on morality. In more modern times Albo has reduced to three the thirteen dogmas of the profession of faith. People are however never wanting whose perverted judgment mistakes the principal for the immaterial and vice versa (11).

The Jewish religion was not the only one to become thus perverted: Christianity has shared the same fate in a much greater degree. Though the Chief principle of its founder was

— 4 —

love, since he even commanded it to one's enemies, his blind followers turned his attemps of reform into a new religion, persecuted the adherents of the Law followed by Christ himself, and inaugurated in his name an era of extermination with Auta de fès etc. (12).

At present the civilised World stands in danger of being infected with the same spirit of perversion under the noble and more novel name of nationalism. It is true that nationalism is a very fruitful idea, since Society is based on the family, which gradually widens to the patriotism of a tribe, city or country, (and just as it is only natural for a father to care for his own child more than for strangers and thus the existence of mankind is made possible so it is easier for a given town or country to take care of their own poor as I have explained in the preface), whereas the socialistic idea of abolishing all local and social differences in an all-absorbing state is an impracticable chimera. But good as this idea is in its legitimate proportions, it becomes a source of danger when abused, just as fire and water, indispenable as they are when regulated, cause havock when let loose. Evidence of this is afforded to us by cultured Germany, where an exaggerated idea of nationalism has led them to acts worthy of the Middle Ages, as the wholesale expulsion of strangers. The noble emperor Frederick of imperishable memory wanted to put a stop to this pernicious kind of nationalism, but untimely death prevented him from giving effect to his enlightened views (13). Nationalism of that sort is so far from improving the situation, but, on the contrary, leads to egotism and atrocities, and is more baneful in its effects than the inquisition, which had at last an excuse in religious fanaticism and might be condoned as a species of madness, whilst intolerant nationalism has no other basis but egotism, in spite of all choice names. We must therefore again express our gratitude to the English for their progress, as proved by the election of a Jew for the third time as Lord Mayor, thus realising the old humanitarian teaching of Moses.

But the idea of nationalism has been spread among some of the civilised Jews, who hope to solve the Jewish question by colonising Palestine, but it is a mistaken idea. It is not only contrary to common sense, as proved in previous pages, it is also against the Mosaical Law. Moses said: "Then the earth is mine and you shall be to me a Kingdom of priests. e. g. our national aim is that of being the spiritual guides of mankind; to preach the monotheistic Idea; to further religious and moral life, but never to form a political dominion or to have national proclivities. We were even partly forbidden the luxury of possessing a King and were taught by our great teacher Moses, that, should we ever feel inclined not to heed his wise precautions and be longing for the possesion of a King like all other nations around us, he be dependent on the prophets who are to be his guides and councillors. He is not even allowed to strengthen his bodyguard by procuring many horses and horsemen, as even the Kings power should not lie in a political but in a spiritual direction. "Neither with might nor with strength but with my spirit saith the Lord" (14). It is always the spiritual Judaism which is surviving all manners of onslaught, whereas material strength is always exposed to all manners of destruction. Whilst all worldly power is transient, the spirit of Judaism is immortal. "The spirit of the Law is your wisdom in the eyes of the nations" (15). Even at the time of the political fall of the nation their only desire was not to retain the shadow of political independence but the freedom to teach and to study the written as well as the oral law, they preferred to remain in the new centres of learning which were developed by them at a time when the national fanatics have sacrificed the flower of the nation to the national Moloch, they preferred to remain in the centre of the diaspora in order to send in all directions where Jews lived dispersed among heathens, who had no notion of humanitarian feelings or morality, rays of Jewish learning and comfort in time of need. This was all the more necessary, considering the fate which befell the ten tribes after the captivity who were swallowed up in a very short time, by the nations surrounding, without being able to fulfill their national mission. Now, our mission being to a certain extent realised, humanitarian wisdom is no more the patrimony of Israel in particular, but became the common good of Humanity in general, our duties will be confined to our being foremost among the nations, or even individuals, who are the standard-bearers of these noble ideas. Our duty is to live in peace with all nations, to be true and faithful to the laws of the lands where we live, to serve our Fatherlands and to sacrifice even our lives for the welfare af our Kings. Then even the Kings will reciprocate these feelings, they will assist us in our intellectual development, as it was expressed by Isaja in the sublime words; "and Kings will be thy Instructors". *(Isaia LIX, 23.)*

But besides these few hints tending towards discouraging us Jews from re-establishing Palestine, we find several passages in the Thalmud where such tendencies are strictly prohibited. The Medrash explanation of Song of Solomon II. 7. "I charge you, O ye daughthers of Jerusalem, by the roes, and by the hinds of the field, that ye stir not up, nor awake **my** love, till she please, is: God made the Jews take three oats (1) they should not hasten the termination of the captivity, (2) they should not rebell against their kings during time of exil, and (3) not to reveal the date of the Millenium (the End קץ (17).

Now, while the first two oats are well understood, the third one is quite unintelligible. We are forbidden or charged not to reveal the day of the Millenium. This charge is quite uncalled for, for the simple reason, that even if we felt the inclination to reveal it, we should be at a loss to know how to do so, as we ourselves labour under the disadvantage of not knowing it. If the Medrash chooses to say in another place. Our father Jacob wished to reveal the day of the Millenium but he immediately forgot it, we might perhaps understand it by assuming Jacob to have been a prophet and supposed to know things which are hidden from other mortals. But why was it necessary to charge the nation at large not to reveal a thing of which they had no notion whatsoever. Evidently the Medrash can only be understood thus. Besides the two first named two oaths we are charged never to' anticipate the Almighty with **Plans** how to bring about the days of the Messiah but must leave even the details of this matter entirely in his hands. We are charged to wait patiently for things to come without any interference whatsoever on our part, and according to this explanation Jacob's intended revelation and his sudden forgetfulness will be understood. Jacob in his endeavour to teach his children the desirability of the continual development of humanity was anxious to describe to them the happy state in which humanity will be when this development will reach the highest degree imaginable, but when he saw with the far sightedness of a Patriarch that human development has no end, he therefore stopped in the middle of his discourse.

And in another place in the Thalmud we find בקש יעקב לגלות הקץ ונסתלקה שכינה הימנו. When Jacob wanted to reveal the Millenium the glory of heaven has departed from him. This shows, that it is very imprudent that the world should await the absolute end of all evil. For the chief point of resemblance of Man to God is, that mortals always know good or evil and have the choice left to themselves. But had they not the option of choosing between right and wrong, good or evil, they were nothing more than cattle and this last state is meant by the "departure of the glory of heaven". But the highest quality of man is that if he betters himself ever so much, there will always be found place to correct and improve his character, and this places him as high if not higher than the Angels.

The Thalmudist Samuel therefore remarked: The difference between our days and the days of the Messiah is only the universal freedom, i. e. that kings will no longer rule the world as heretofore, when they could do with a man as they liked that they were when at liberty to deprive him of his life and freedom at their pleasure as one deals with his cattle. The learned Rambam (Maimonides) also adheres to this idea, so that the whole only intends to the realization of the words: "And the earth will be full of "knowledge as the waters cover the sea". The ruling and dominion of the Almighty shall be acknowledged by the whole of the world and we Jews will be justly proud to have been the founders of this great idea and may look forward to a time when all mankind will live in peace, concord and union and love each other, this being the chief principles of the Jewish Religion and its two elements. Thus this highest degree of nationalism can only be manifested by our love to each other and by our trying to establish places, where we are able to enjoy and educate and instruct our fellowmen in the highly moral principles of our holy scripture and the Thalmud, and by supporting one another materially where such support is needed. One of the principle aims in view would be that the workingmen should have a place where they could apply for a situation, and a register of vacant places be constantly kept so that they should not want to linger about in the streets, especially those who have just only immigrated to this country and are ignorant of the language. Then to instruct our workingmen properly in reading and writing so that they need not spend their leisure hours about the public and gambling houses, where they lose their scanty but hard earnings.

True Nationalism teaches that every nation should endeavour to study its own faults and try to ameliorate and avoid them, thus freeing themselves from evil, gaining and deserving the love of all mankind.

But you must not think, dear Readers, that I mean to advocate assimilation, that we should mix ourselves between and with other nations. No, this is not my idea, Since I cannot agree with the fanaticism of one creed I am not likely to recommend that of another. Just as a Russian politician and philosopher Wladimir Solowiew wrote once to the Synode when speaking of the Jewish question "The Jewish question" said he „will never be settled as long as the question about yourselves is not decided upon. One holds with the Slavians another with the Catholics a third with the Protestants ect. just as in Africa there are many sects of Muselmen. When the world will reach that standard that all will understand the two chief principles of belief, you will have no need of asking how this question will be settled as it will be settled by itself.".

Thus if every nation will try and endeavour to propagate humanity and love to fellowmen, we will not only have true and real nationalism, but at the same time also answer the question of the freethinkers who ask: "Why should I subject myself to criticism and hold with the Jews, if I am a free-thinker"? If we are so far advanced as to feel the absolute necessity of love to kinship and fellowmen, the world will surely become united. If we Jews have commenced educating the world and ourselves in high human and moral principles, let us not now neglect it in its very infancy. We must try to support mankind morally and materially in every way so as to fulfil the holy words: "Israel, I shall be gloryfied through thee", that the world should love and esteem, not despise us.

We Jews are like a Company of explorers going through wilderness and dangers to discover far off lands for the benefit of humanity, having attained their object, their duty is clearly not to seperate but to stick together till the end.

We Jews must never think of Nationalism in a political sense. For what is the use of it as long as the world is not united? as long as one will fight against his fellowman? as long as one is affraid of his neighbour? But if we leave out the political point, when the world becomes united in all respects, why then should you need a special fatherland? Does not an old proverb say "Ubi bene ibi patria" or "Where it is good there is the fatherland"? But, dear Readers, you must not think I am in any way against the Colonisation of Palestine. I think the idea of colonising Palestine very good and practical, but I cannot approve of the ways and means taken to its realisation. It must and can never be done out of charity or weekly collection. I highly esteem the idea itself, provided, certainly, that the children of the colonists will devote themselves to thoroughly study the Hebrew language and recall it to life again.

For if even there are now the Volapüc and Esperand languages, which are intended to become universal and are much easier to learn than the Hebrew, yet this language no doubt deserves ours highest esteem and preference to all others, because in this language Moses and the Prophets have spoken to the people and taught them those high morals and sublime human ideas of which the whole world is proud after thousands of years and always will be so. It thus becomes to us the dearest and most valuable living memorial of the time gone by, much dearer than all costly monuments erected by other nations to their heros, who brought out thousands of people to the field of battle, where they lost their lives, a memorial of horror and cruelty. Our intention is quite to the contrary, viz. to propagate a spiritual reign in the World in the quiet and most peacefull way as the Prophets Isaiah and Michah said "And I will turn their swords into sickles" etc., that there will be no more war in the world". To commemorate this idea we erect a living memorial, in supporting the colonists and cultivating the Hebrew language. But my advice is not to establish these monuments by way of charity because to provide for one colonist we should want as much as £300 or £400 whilst we could with this capital help many families amongst us. I am quite sure that many a family is well helped with a Loan of one Pound or so. I did once prove this in my native country in the city of Petrokow (Russian-Poland) that a man can, with but a trifling support, do much more than by Colonisation.

Agriculture being the principal and most useful means of livelihood in the world(18),though it cannot lead to great riches, is very necessary, and it is nothing but our duty to help those who would like to devote themselves to tilling the ground. But this can only be successfully gained, if we establish Companies on shares, repayable after a certain limit of time with 2 percent to 6 percent interest, part of which should go towards a drawing which can be held, say, twice a year. It would also be possible to issue small shares divided in parts, so as to enable the less wealthy to purchase them, and I am sure they will sell very well.—

Thus a large sum can be obtained to provide land for agriculturists, and when this expended, new series of shares can be issued etc. In this way ground can be acquired in Palestine and other places to settle colonists thereon, who should educate their children giving them a thorough knowledge of Hebrew and the high morals of religion. They must also be taught Volapűc or Esperand which will connect and unite the whole world and one will no more be looked upon like a stranger as the Prophet Zephania says אז אהפוך אל עמים שפה ברורה לקרא כולם בשם ה' לעברו שכם אחר. (For then I will turn unto people pure language that they may all call upon the name of the Lord to serve him with one consent, *Zephania III. 9.*) that they will all speak an understandable language which will lead them to a perfect spiritual union in knowing and acknowledging the might of God.

But you must not be surprised that I advise to colonise

also other places, for we find even in the Thalmud עתידה ארץ ישראל שתתפשט בכל העולם "The Land of Israel will extend over all the world" i. e. that the high human principles of morality which we have been taught in Palestine will be propagated throughout all the World (19). And basing on the words of Michah: And all the nations will love Palestine and go hither, for from Zion comes the law and the word of God from Jerusalem" this would be the best monument we can erect for all times and generations.

It would be very good, I say, to erect such an eternal monument, but I would never advise to depend on futile ideas and imaginations, for my explanation and way of reasoning is one agreeing fully with philosophy and religion. And we can hope that the greatest advantage will arise of it to the world, if we only try to propagate humanity, as the Prophet Habakuk says: "And the earth will be full of knowledge as the water covers the sea", to what we can add as a consequence the words of Joel: "Hereafter I will pour out my spirit upon all flesh" and the words of Isiah "The glory of god will be revealed and all flesh will acknowledge it together". We need not be hated by any class or sect of the human race as long as we try and endeavour to propagate humanity and love within us, as the Prophet Isaia says: זה יאמר לה' אני וכו' "One will say I am the Lord's, and another shall call himself by the name of Jacob, and another shall subscribe with his hand unto the Lord and surname himself by the name of Israel"(*Isiah XLIV 5*) that there will be different sects, each of which will think different but that such an arrangement will be a blessing for all. For through this we will be able to come to a perfect union, freeing ourselves from every fanaticism, little by little, so that we will at last reach that standard, of which Moses speaks before giving us God's ten Commandements: "And ye shall be unto Me a beloved nation from all other nations for Mine is all the earth". והייתם לי סגולה מכל העמים כי לי כל הארץ meaning that Israel will be an example for all other nations and lands which God equally loves.

I will here repeat again, we Jews must sincerely congratulate the English nobility that they have reached such a standard of gentleness as I have spoken of, but I shall ask you to kindly excuse me if I will point out a few still existing faults. We know that if even the world will exist for thousands of years we will always find something to amend and improve, for there is no limit to science and no end to perfection of humanity. It may also be possible, that these faults are not known to you and you can therefore not understand how bad and injurious they are. In the first place I will mention the fighting in the open street. It is shameful to see two grown up persons settling their differences commercial or private, by way of fight.

The word "fight" is so holy amongst the lower class, that they feel no shame or disgrace for their actions, and the police being used to it, do not take the trouble to interfere, and certainly it is not a moral or human sight for our children fo see. It does not improve the morals of the public and it puts me in mind of the middle ages in Rome when wild beasts used to be put in the arena to fight with man, and then again if a man asks another to fight it would be a disgrace for the other to refuse, thus the hospitals are kept busy and it is a pretext for thieving. The most striking feature is that sometimes the severely, nay fatally injured party, owing to the difficulty of bringing the offenderto justice, stands a doubtful chance of getting his right by way of law. We may unfortunately often see a poor traveller, who earns his bread with the sweat of his brow surrounded by a swarm of blackguards who throw stones at him, lay hand on his goods and property, knock him about and deprive him of his substance, brutally injuring his health, sometimes nearly or totally injuring him.

Those boys who are by no one prevented in their evil doing, having no moral principles implanted into their hearts in their infancy, become as wild as beasts, and if they grow up, they are but thieves and murderers. They know not, they have never been taught to respect anyone and as soon as they catch sight of somebody, whose appearance they do not quite like, immediately a rush is made at him and he is being illtreated in a most abhorrent and dispisable way. Especially when they notice a stranger, an old man, a foreigner of whom they know that he is unable to understand and answer to their vulgar and abusive slang, this man is hardly sure of his property and person. In every other civilised or even only partly advanced and enlightened country, we will find boys highly respecting and strictly taught at school and home to show regard to elder people because of their age and experience and especially to a stranger, because he is strange to the languge and customs of the country. Unfortunately we notice quite the reverse in England which boast to be more advanced in civilisation than any other european state. Here the boy therefore takes advantage of his artificial fist defence in illegal purposes, and brings this with him from the school into his private and public life.

The teachers ought to teach the children moral principles and if the teacher finds that a boy misbehaves himself when out from school, the boy ought to be punished for it, also that every boy should guard the morals of the other, and the teacher by giving prices to those who inform to the bad behaving of the other boys out of the schools.

Although England is a free land still one has no right to shoot in public as he may do injury to another the same aught to be with the boys, they may be allowed to enjoy themselves but not to injure anyone, therefore my idea is that there can never be an end until fighting is totally abolished, not that they should take the law in their own hands, we pay the judges for that.

Why if we look at Moses, we will see that, when still a mere boy, he saw an Egyptian illtreating his brother, he became so excited that under the impulse of the moment, he has committed a crime, for which he could pay with his life. He was not at all nervous or soft hearted, for we observe what he had to suffer and to stand, what troubles he had to endure at the head of his nation, but the sight of cruelty made him forget himself and, disgusted by the impression, he became guilty of murder, he endangered his own life. Our Rabbis also teach us: "Who ever lifts up his hand against his fellowman to injure him is a wicked and unworthy man". I therefore hope that our gentle and influential citizens will endeavour to banish this disgraceful custom from their midst, that they will find a way to have the boys taught morals of life and behaviour, that they will influence the teachers and spiritual guides of the young generation to command their pupils to leave off fighting at all, and punish severely anyone who will disobey such command.

In conclusion I must humbly ask our noble brethren, with their kind permission, that they shall pay more strict attention to the management of their Benevolent Institutions. They spend and contribute a great deal of money towards these Institutions every year, but, they cannot have always at the head of these Institutions such men, who are thoroughly acquainted with the position of our poorer brethren, and who should recognise a really deserving case, wanting immediate attention. It is very seldom the case, that a really deserving person is duly attended to, since the investigating officers are already quite used to the bitter cry of need and poverty, and thereby do very little care to listen to really deserving persons and to become impressed by the details put before them. Their rules are quite bare of strict principles, so that if one wishes to enjoy the privelege of their support, it, in the long run, costs him more time and money than the support is worth.

I will illustrate this by just one case, which happened to come especially under my notice. Here is an Orphan Asylum called "Neveh-Zedek", where children are taken in by votes of members. I happened to know a poor striving widow, whose child was well deserving support. Since she had no acquaintance with any members of that institution, she had to advertise in the papers for votes, this entailing an expense of 16/- besides petty expenses. After all, her endeavours proved a failure, and not only has she attained nothing good, but the expense in the hope of bettering her poor child's future, has devoured her only and small capital and ruined her entirely. I think, in such cases it would be quite sufficient, that parents should make an application to the Authorities in writing, and this application be subject to a thorough investigation. I should therefore request the Committees of Benevolent Institutions, that when considering an application for relief, care should be taken to distinguish a deserving case when exception should sometimes be made to the general rules especially if a case is introduced by a Warden of a Synagogue or other authority. Our Rabbis say: "Whoever gives right judgement in case in its perfect truth, he makes the glory of God rest in the midst of the nation, for it says, God rests within the Congregation of the just" כל הדן דין אמת לאמיתו" משרה שכינה בישראל דכתיב אלהים נצב בעדת אל. In another place it says that he is a partner to God and helps to support the world.

Thus we see that a judge can even give right judgement in a case, but he can and must not place himself in the position, in which the accused may have been whilst doing wrong, for if the judge did so, he would always be able to find enough reason to discharge him. For we know, that whatever a man will never do under ordinary circumstances, he is compelled to commit by fate or some circumstances of life or lastly under the impuls of the moment.

I also wish to advice you not to spend so much money on the Synagogues and their adornment. The principal is "large and simple". For we find in the Thalmud: Two of our Rabbis, (it says there Rav Hama Bar Hanina and Rav Ashia Rabba) went past the Synagogue in Lud which was a beautiful building. The former said to the latter: "How much money have our ancestors spent on this building", whereupon the latter answered: "How many lives costs this building" meaning how many could be supported of these funds, (*Shekalim 19*), especially learned men worthy of support. The Rabbis also say in one place: "What fools are human beings, who respect many scrolls of law and disregard great poeple.

I again express my gratitude to the English nobility who promote humanity with all efforts. I also am thankful to the Emperor Francis Joseph of Austria, who with indefatigable efforts tries to implant human feelings in the hearts of his subjects and bravely fights against antisemitism. Those countries who persecute the Jews, because of the wicked and unjust amongst them, institute special law and limitation of their rights, such lands act very wrongly in so doing, for there is not a single nation, that should consist of any rigtheous members and have no evildoers in their midst. But it is a law of nature that "one will sooner see a hair in his neighbours eye than a board in his own", and so it is easier to take notice of somebody else's oversight than cf one's own sin, and should one even notice a fault of his own he looks upon it as a trifling matter whilst errors of others are looked upon through a microscope and seem far greater than they really are.

It is also a very wrong and unjust idea with mankind to blame a whole nation for the wrong of one single individual, Moses asked of the Almighty: "If one man sinneth will thou be wroth on all the congregation?" איש אחד יחטא ועל כל העדה תקצוף? — We must after all not forget, that a great many of faults and the dishonesty existing amongst the Jews, is not a fault of their own, but has been brought about by their neighbours themselves. Jews having been shut out from every means of earning a honest livelihood and having only to satisfy themselves by living upon uuconstant and futile undertakings have been forced to cheat and defraud their neighbours. Do not we all know that the principal point of commerce is to dazzle the eyes of the buyer, and if we only look for one moment upon England's commerce at large, will we not clearly see that it is only founded to dazzling and blinding the eyes of the costumer? Why Kings and sovereign's policy is only a means to blind a neighbours eyes and entails more dangers than commerce. Thus, the more limiting rights and laws we creat, the more do we induce them to transgress these laws.

The only way to improve these great evil is, to give equal rights and privileges to all citizens, where one will not have to fear or dread, to avoid or shun his fellowmen. We see clearly that in such lands where Jews are equally priviledged with all citizens, they give the Government no reason whatever to complain about them, they are honest, true and loyal subjects, good and faithful citizens, loving their fellowmen, and duly esteeming the heads of the Government.

In order as to promote improvement of humanity amongst the Jews, 1 could advise, that no obstacles shall be put in the way of the Jews and permission be forthwith given to them, upon their request, to establish Societies and unions with a view to support their fellowmen, not as it happens in other countries, that replies to such motions are usually laid ad acta, or, that after a score or more years waiting they are totally refused.

As an instance of the latter we can mention that in one country Jews only after long years waiting obtained Permission to open a Reading and Lecture Hall only at their Synagogue. Such actions prevent greatly the advance of civilization, for in Synagogues strict orthodoxy is observed' and those who would like to be more advanced have no room there and no other meeting place, they are thus totally prevented from coming forward and propagating good and healthy ideas.

It is also very unwise and unreasonable, that especially in Russia, one can now-a-days not depend on the police for ful protection of his person and property. The police officials are very covetous and do therefore hold only with the rich, seeking for every opportunity to oppress and deprive the poor. They also do not pay the slightest attention to thieves, who give them a certain share of every successful booty. Their eyes are only watching the honest poeple whom they are anxious to catch in their trap. Amongst the laws of several countries, especially Russia, one finds such, that are still a remnant of the middle ages. How ridiculous is for instance the law, that every one must be provided with a passport, to be produced when travelling from one town to another, from one village to a neighbouring one. If we will for one moment only consider the difficulties and obstacles put in our way, before we ultimately get that passport, a matter of great formality, trouble and substantial cost, we will at once see how ridiculous it is and what it is intended to. Now it is marvellous with what peculiar severity the subordinate police officials are hunting to controll these passports. Suppose a merchant, having a great many things to think of, being in a hurry, forgets to take his document with him and upon the investigation of the officials, late at night, is found without one, he, be he whoever he is, is liable to be arrested, dragged to the Police Station and is usually sent by étape (all the way on foot) to the place whence he came, in company with thieves and other notorious criminals. But this happens only with honest and straightforward people, whilst a thief is usually provided with a score of Passports and lives on friendly terms with the police officers. There are, besides, many statutes of law, that require alteration in the spirit of the present age.

but space does not permit me to specify them. Although those laws refer to Jew and gentile alike. yet, the Jews who must only depend on commerce find most occasion to break such law, and feel thus most bitterly the consequences.

It is extremely foolish on the part of Gentiles to despise and hate the Jews because of those amongst them who are morally corrupt wicked and evildoing. They seem not to know that the Jews themselves despise such people more because they bring shame and degradation upon the whole nation of Israel. But, we find such wicked and corrupt persons in every nation and every creed and should therefore not blame the Jews because of a few excentions unworthy of the name and nation they represent. And besides these few are helped and supported by the police. Many times, I have spoken on this subject to several very influential Gentlemen asking them to assist me in putting a limit to the dishonest dealings amongst the Jews and their neighbours, but they declined, by reason of the officials having a part in the booty. There is therefore no other and better advice than to ask the Government to interfere and enable its subjects to educate themselves morally and to thoroughly study and acquire the principles of true humanity, that humane Societies shall be established everywhere, which should try to stop dishonest dealings between man and man and support the needy morally and materially. If this will be done, outrages against law and government will be prevented. Let me give one instance:

Owing to excessive smuggling of foreign goods, Russia has issued an edict, limiting the pale of the Jewish settlement to 50 werst from every frontier. At the same time, having a thorough experience in the commercial ways of those parts of Russia and Russian-Poland, I can only say, that those who occupy themselves with smuggling are of much more disadvantage to the Jewish merchants, not only of the frontier and its neighbourhood, and even to Jewish merchants in general, than to the Governement. The law requires that every kind of goods and articles shall have a mark (plombe), and as such sign or mark, can come off in the long run, either owing to the goods being in stock for a long time or to their being returned by the purchaser or other reason, the police and custom officers finding a piece of stuff without the due mark, confiscate the whole stock without distinction and the trouble to get these goods back is great, costly and takes years.

What can the poor Jews help against such dealing, when the smugglers are helped and assisted in their work by the bribed officials, and the more officers the more smugglers we see? Nothing can prevent such an horrible state, bare the establishment of the humane society I spoke of before, which will take care to show up all disadvantages arising of this evil.

It is a real chance coincidence, that when writing these lines I can commemorate the Mass Meeting called and presided over by the Right Hon. the Lord Mayor of London "on the treatment of the Jews in Rusia". It has been said at this Meeting that the Emperor of Russia can impossibly be aware of the particulars how things are going on in his vast empire. I am really thankful to these noble Gentlemen, for they have hit the right point. I know it for an established fact, nay it costed me great trouble and exertions to learn that not only the Emperor but even the governors of the frontier provinces are positively unaware of the state of things. When I was at home, I earnestly urged upon a few noble gentlemen to reveal the particulars of the facts to the administrative powers, but they answered me that since they would not like to go against a great many of government officials, who are each one and all bribed, in order that they should make themselves overlook the fact, and since things do not hurt them at all, they do not see their way clear to interfere. It would therefore be my pleasant duty to ask of those noble Gentlemen, who have kindly taken upon themselves to present a Memorial to the Russian Emperor on behalf of the Jews, that when they reveal to him the true state of things in his vast empire, they should also bring before him my motion about the establishment of humane societies, such as I have described above, as the only way and means, which will most speedily put an end to abominable transgressions against law, country and crown, whereby the whole nation is ruining itself by degrees. It will be advisable, that such humane Societies, when established, should have the absolute power to form such beneficial unions, as they will consider necessary for the promotion of common health and universal happiness. When this is done, not only will the whole nation breathe free and happy, not only all obstacles will be removed, which now make Russia an unhappy land, and its subject a miserable burden to that country, but we will also attain a great aim, so far away from within our reach to day. We will shut up the mouths of all the Jew-haters and Jew-eaters, who are constantly sharpening their teeth to find new faults with their Jewish fellow citizens. It is our first and imperative duty to make them shut up, as our well-wishers do not see great faults with our Russian Brethren even now, in a crisis of hatred and persecution, need, suffering and misery.

Proofs of this we can find in the works of Prince Demidoff St. Donato "The Jewish question in Russia" (translated into English by I. Michael H. M. Consul in St. Petersbourg) the Archimandrit Nikanor of Odessa and others. As to those whose pleasure it is always to criticise and to blame, we cannot take notice of them, and will never get rid of their false conclusions, as they will always find something to say against us, something to criticise in our actions, behaviour, dealings etc.

That the Jews were always wrongly blamed by their enemies, was sufficiently proved in a speech of Dr. Bloch, delivered in the Austrian Parliament during the sittings in February 1890. This is the extract:—

„There are many in our nation, whom the Jews can „never satisfy, however they would do. In Austria we hear „a complaint, that the public schools are overcrowded with „Jewish children, while on the other hand they gramble „in Galizia, that a too small number of Jews send their „children to educational institutions If a Jew is generous „and liberal, spending a great deal of his money in every „respect, he is accused of prodigality and extravagancy, „or hunting after pleasures, whilst if he lives economising „wherever he can and leads a modest life, they grumble at „his avarice and he is looked upon as a miser. Does he „abstain himself from interfering in politics, they say, „he has no feelings for his native land, he has no love „for his mother country, whilst if he sticks to a political

„league, trying to bravely defend its cause, he is pointed „at as one who likes to interfere everywhere. If he shows „loyalty, sympathising with the government, they say, „he holds always only with the stronger party, with the „mightier power, whilst if he joins the liberals and opposes „government, they grumble, that the Jew can only over- „throw every good plan and will never assist a good cause".

If we now look upon Russia, we will observe just the same. In former times, one always heard a complaint that the Jews do not send their children to school, they do not like to work and will never take to a trade or profession, keeping only to commerce in its different styles. Now they are being persecuted, driven out from their homes and property, their rights and privileges are limited day by day, because they have devoted themselves too much to education, they have too many learned men, too many good artisans, they have overcrowded every trade, overfilled every profession.

But leaving all that on one side, let us now investigate some other faults which the enemies of the nation of Israel find with the Jews.

Some say, the Jews deprive their gentile neighbours of a livelihood, and yet, we see that where, in opposition to Jewish shops, christians have established the same stores, with a view of benefitting their customers by selling goods under cost price, yet the buyers stick to the Jew, who, speculating on one hand, and economising in his wants on the other, limits his profits to the minimum and can thus sell his goods much cheaper than his gentile neighbour. Where again, Jews are buying goods of Gentiles, the sellers realise the highest prices, since, as nearly all Jews are excluded from trades, they must live from hand to mouth, and there are always many anxious to buy one article, and one tries therefore to offer a higher price than the other, so that, when finally the goods are sold to the highest bidder, they leave the buyer only a very small profit

From others we may often hear, Jews are usurers, lend money on unreasonable interest etc. Now I happen to know a great many, whom this profession has entirely ruined, as they lent their monies away and never had the chance of seeing them again, neither capital nor interest, and then, I really fail to see, how we can now-a-days wonder seeing a Jew, who, when he risks all his money, wishes to make at least a good profit by it, if we see, that those, who lend away articles or sell them on "hire system", when the article is the property of the seller so long, until the whole sum agreed is paid up in full, and where, suppose the last two instalments are not paid within as many as 3 weeks only, all previous payments are forfeited, the agreement void, and the property returns to the seller.

If such dealing, with a profit of 200 or 300 per cent is justifiable, surely the Jew is not wrong at all.

We meet again others who say: the Jewish publicans make of their gentile fellowmen drunkards. Now do we not find many nay too many drunkards in such towns where there is no Jewish publican. Here in England, for instance, where only one of every thousand public houses belongs to a Jew, and where spirits are so dear, are we short of drunkards? Have we not enough and more than enough, and do we ever find any Jews amongst them.

This, I think, will sufficiently, prove, how wrong it is of our "every day criticisers" to ascribe such incredible faults to the Jews.

A further proof how Jews will never succeed in pacifying their enemies we find, if we remind ourselves of the accusation brought against the Jews about their using human blood for Passover (עלילת הדם). We all know how severely we are prohibited to use meat that has not been soaked in water for at least ½ hour, how it then lies in salt for an hour and is washed again to remove the last trace of blood from it. We also know, that a Jew is not permitted to use an egg, if the least bloodstain be found in it. Now especially human blood. Is not the use of it repeatedly forbidden in a most decided manner in the Holy Writ? Does it not say: "כי הדם היא הנפש" "For the blood is the soul"! Have not non-jewish clergymen, nay even Popes, already taken a holy oath and given their assurance to testify, that the accusation, that the Jews even only intend to use human blood, is ridiculous and false? Have not great men of science, great statesmen, publicly expressed their indignation on hearing such charges brought forward? And yet, in the XIX century, there are still such men, and men professing to be educated, who do not shrink from bringing such false charge, and persecuting the Jews or allowing them to be persecuted by the poeple for a crime they never thought of committing.

Our enemies will thus never be satisfied with us, and, I think, how wisely did our Rabbis teach us: רבי אומר איזו היא דרך ישרה שיבור לו האדם כל שהיא תפארת לעשיה ותפארת לו מן האדם. (Aboth II, 1.) "Which is the rigth course a man should choose for himfelf? That which he feels to be honourable to himself, and which brings him honour from every noble man". ("האדם. noble man as explained in the preface.)

Now, our great moralists (?) accuse the Jews, especially

those, who come over to England of bad habits and corrupt character. As a matter of fact, the noble Englishman can impossibly wonder if he finds amongst those of our foreign Brethren whom he sees in England, such, whose character is corrupt and who do not shrink before a transgression of law. For we must consider, that many who come over to this country from Russia, with exceptions of course, are either such, as have hitherto led a vicious course of life, and were therefore compelled to leave their homes, or freethinkers, whose sense and understanding has not yet quite developed itself. The better class of people remain at their homes, notwithstanding the great sufferings they have to endure. The orthodox Jews, who comprise the greatest part of the Jewish population, and who, one and all, are well and thoroughly educated, brought up in pure moral and humane principles which they always show. In their commercial relations they are as their gentile neighbours, and give way to speculation and profits only, when prompted to do so by circumstances of life. Otherwise their life is devoted to study of law and charitable deeds.

We must therefore not wonder if amongst those whom we see here we can find such with corrupt moral character. We expect them to be such, but even this falls back upon our wealthier brethren, who by not providing a place for their poorer brethren, where they should meet and improve and support each other morally and materially, have forced them to remain as they were, nay, to become still worse.

Had such place been thought of, we would surely not meet with wicked men amidst our Brethren, nor would the Socialistic idea have found so many blind followers, as it has gained now-a-days. May I therefore ask those of my noble readers, who feel themselves able to do so, that they should kindly pay due attention to this fault and try their utmost to amend it for the good of our nation and for humanity's sake.

It would also be necessary to urge upon our noble Brethren that they should take a greater interest in the labour question.

Those of our poor Brethren who live in such parts of the Globe, where they must suffer under persecution and government oppression by certain bye-laws, limiting their rights and privileges enclosing them in a ghetto, where they have to submit to privation in every way, and are exposed to uncredible need and misery, I would heartily advise to be tolerant to show themselves brave and patiently submit to everything put upon them, difficult as it may be.

Such tyranical laws and restrictions are like a pestilence, like an infectious disease, which, though severe, cannot be of long duration. We find in the Thalmud *(Jebamoth p. 21)* that Rabbi Gamliel has once deplored the wreck of a ship, which amongst other passengers included the great Rabbi Akiba. The latter, when saved, told his faithful friend that he miraculously saw a board floating and, taking refuge on this board, he used to bow his head to every wave which rolled by.

"Hence we learn" say our sages, "that when the wicked oppress a man, he shall bow his head unto them". We find the same is told of Rabbi Meir (ibid.) who relating his rescue says: "One wave transmitted me to the other, that to the next one, until I thus reach dry land". I hope every man with common sense will understand in these allegorical descriptions but a moral teaching to us to be tolerant towards our enemies and to patiently bear every injustice done to us. Our oppressed and persecuted Brethren in Russia and elsewhere must not lose their courage, but on the contrary, bravely submit to all, try to keep the letter of the laws, never transgressing them in the least and seek consolation in their loyalty towards their superiors and in the good hope for better days to come.

Acting in this way, they will, though never closing the mouths of their enemies, yet on the other hand by their mute tolerance, turn upon themselves the eyes of the Rulers and noble men of those countries of the habitable globe, where humanity and civilization has reached a high standard as the Queen of England, the Kings of Austria, Germany, Italy, the Heads of France, the United States and other governments, and they, by their influential support and interference, will endeavour to soften the hearts, to enlighten the minds of the oppressors, to open their eyes on all subjects, which may be either concealed from them or misrepresented to them, and destroying all hatred and enmity, spread peace and welfare everywhere, thus realising the words of Isaiah והיו מלכים אומניך "And Kings will be thy nursing fathers" (LXIX 23). And as we have been taught by our Rabbis "to pray for the welfare of the Kings" as will they promote our happiness and unite all the universe in peace, as our Psalmist says: למען אחי ורעי אדברה נא שלום בך "For the sake of my Brethren and friends will I speak of peace unto thee". And in fact, nothing can so well promote the happiness of the world as peace, as our Rabbis teach us: לא מצא הקב"ה כלי מחזיק ברכה לישראל אלא השלום שנאמר ה' עוז לעמו יתן ה' יברך את עמו בשלום. The Almighty has found no better way and means to bring blessings to Israel but peace, as it says: "God will give strength unto His people, blessing them with peace".

NOTES.

Before I commence to explain a few passages in this work, may I be allowed to quote a few Rules on which my theory is based.

Rule 1.— In some places of the Pentateuch we will find that the words are not clearly explained, but that what is wanted in one place, is explained in another.

Rule 2.—Many times a verse consists of two parts, speaking of two different subjects, both being afterwards seperately explained. Often we will find also the reverse, that is that both subjects are explained collectively owing to a special motive.

Rule 3.—A verse in the Holy Scripture can often be explained in many ways, some even opposed and contradicting each other. We must, therefore not be surprised, if one studying the Books of Moses will arrive at conclusions, which will very much differ from those, made by another as arduous a student. This difference of opinions, views and conclusions drawn of the same subject is striking not only considering single individuals, but we will observe that these views and opinions differ greatly in every generation, and at last there will be as much reason for one opinion as there will be sufficient motive to justify another, even quite the opposed theory. The orthodox will as bravely fight for the truth of his conclusions, as will the more advanced philosopher find sufficient ground to prove his ideas of the same verse, basing on and guided by certain words in a text. But it is clear that our great Legislator had been obliged to speak allegorically, for he knew that different as the faces and features of men, are their opinions, understandings, ideas and views.

(1).—A proof that we cannot love God without feeling sincere love for and sympathy with our fellow creatures, we will find in our Ten Commandments, the sole basis of our holy creed. In the first commandment we read:— "I am the Lord thy God who hath brought thee out of the land of Egypt, out of the house of bondage". Why does it not say: "Who has created the Heaven and Earth and all thereon?" This tends to prove, that since God so miraculeously delivered them from the land of Egypt, where they were treated like Slaves, since he has shown them so strikingly His abundant mercy and love, He wishes the Israelites to learn to be loving, kind and merciful to their fellowmen, the poor and the oppressed and this means, "to know and love God". Just so in the second commandment, which concludes with the words: "Who bestoweth gracious favours upon those who love Me unto the thousandth generation". Here He speaks of those who keep His commandments as such who love Him.

In the third commandment we find the way given, by which judges are enabled to give right judgment in every case. We are commanded again to keep the Sabbath day. "Thou shalt do no work whatever", it says, "nor thy son, nor thy daughter, nor thy man servant, nor thy maid-servant, nor thy cattle or thy stranger in thy gates". But why the seventh day? Because in 6 days God hath created heaven and earth, the sea and all therein. All modern philosophers agree that six periods have elapsed, before man has been able to exist on the habitable globe. "Therefore" continues the commandment "God hath blessed the seventh day and made it holy". If we compare the text of the Ten Commandments in Exodus to that of their repetition in Deutronomy, we will find that in both different reasons are given for the sanctification of the Sabbath.

In Exodus the principal stress is laid on "God created Heaven and Earth" what has hitherto not been mentioned in the עשרת הדברות at all, and why it is expressly the seventh day that we must keep holy. In Deutronomy we see as reason of keeping the Sabbath holy "that thy man servant and thy maid servant shall rest like unto thee, and thou shalt remember that thou hast been a slave in the land of Egypt and God hath brought thee out from there, therefore He hath commanded to keep the Sabbath". This accounts for what our Rabbis say זכור ושמור בדבור אחד נאמרו", i. e. that both the texts of the Ten Commandments, have to be regarded as one sentence. They are unimaginable when separated and can only be explained if closely connected with each other. I need hardly continue to point out, how the rest of the ten Commandments aim simultanously at love of man, as every one of my readers will doubtless understand, that each Commandment bids us to show our sincerest love to our fellowmen in so decided a manner, that there cannot be the slightest doubt about it.

We also find (Deutr. X, 18) עשה משפט יתום ואלמנה ואוהב גר לתת לו לחם ושמלה ואהבתם את הגר וכו' את ה' אלהיך תירא אותו תעבוד ובו תדבק "He doth execute the judgement of the fatherless and widow, and loveth the stranger etc., love ye therefore the stranger etc. Thou shalt fear the Lord thy God, Him shalt thou serve and to Him shalt thou cleave etc." In Deutr. XI, 22, לאהבה את ה' אלהיכם ללכת בדרכיו ולדבקה בו "to love your God, to walk in his ways and to cleave unto Him". Speaking of this verse our Rabbis ask: How can one cleave to his creator? and answer: but by learning to walk in his ways and to imitate His abundant high qualities, being merciful as He is, bestowing favours as he does מה הוא רחום אף אתה רחום מה הוא חנון אף אתה חנון Thus our great Legislator starts by specyfying the great qualities of the Almighty and inducing us to imitate them and finishes that by so doing we will love our God and cleave unto him.

(2). It is impossible to love mankind without truly feeling love and reverence for our God. We find in Jeremiah XXII 15-16 ואביך הלא אכל ושתה ועשה משפט וצדקה אז טוב לו. דן דין עני ואביון אז טוב לו הלא הוא הדעה אתי נאום ה'. "Did not thy father eat and drink and do judgment and justice and then it was well to him? He judged the cause of the poor and needy, then it was well to him. Is not this to know Me? saith the Lord". Here we find a specification o qualities by learning which a man gains true love to God and knowledge of his Maker on high. We find further in the Talmud: (Brachoth 63) דרש בר קפרא — איזו הוא פרשה קטנה שכל גופי התורה תלוים בה שנאמר בכל דרכיך דעהו והוא יישר אורהותיך (משלי ג 6). Which is the shortest sentence including the principal basis of our holy law, it says "in all thy ways know Him and He will straighten thy path". Thus if we do all that is good, humane and beneficial to mankind we learn to know our Creator to love Him truly and sincerely.

Frontlets תפלין and fringes ציצת which we are commanded to wear do also clearly remind us of the connection existing between love of God and love of man. With regard to תפלין the Ebn Esra and the Rashbam have already given a most detailed explanation in this respect, and I need not coment upon it here. They pointed to the words כתבם על לוח לבך Write them upon the tablets of thy heart and showed that, if we truly comprehend the high morals enclosed in the commandment of תפילין we have to learn from it, that neither shall our heart ever consent, our hand ever do, nor shall our eyes ever dare to look upon anything that is wrong. Hereto we may add that since in the first chapter of שמע it says: "יהיו הדברים האלה אשר אנכי מצוך היום על לבביך" "And the words I command thee this day shall be upon thy heart", and in the second: "ושמתם את דברי אלה על לבבכם" "And you shall put these My words upon your hearts", it means that we have to thoroughly study the words of God and inscribe them into our heart as a constant guide of our actions towards our fellowmen.

A pamphlet on the subject when frontlets have been first introduced has been published not long ago by Mr. Rodkinson.

With regard to fringes ציצית it seems to me that since at that time people did not know of trousers as a wearing apparel, they used to cover themselves with long garments and in order as to warrant to the future generations the full preservation of their bodily health, as also to introduce principles of morality and chastity, our great Legislator has commanded in the name of God (Deutr. XXII, 12) גדלים תעשה לך על ארבע כנפות כסותך אשר תכסה בה. Thou shalt make thee fringes upon the four quarters of thy vesture wherewith thou coverest thyself, Moses had, in order as to bind his hearers to fulfill his commandments aiming at the moral improvement of his beloved nation, been obliged to speak in the name of the Almighty as an express commandment, or else they would not make it their duty to obey. And as he, Moses, has thoroughly felt, that the love of God and the love of man is very closely connected, and that man is only "man in full" when he has his godly gift, his senses and feelings, this precious צלם אלהים impressed upon him, the great legislator commanded to chose the blue colour תכלת as the nearest to heavenly colour, and reminding us constantly of our great and merciful father in Heaven.

I must clearly point out that I am far from intending to dissuade any one חלילה from the use of fringes and frontlets. I only wish to express my opinion about how our great legislator came to give these commandments, so as to obtain the freethinking class of our Brethren to regard it as fanaticism and to present it to the true believers as a natural command. I refer also to the words, with which the great Ebn Esra finishes his explanation about this subject: דברי חכמים אין צריכין חיזוק. "The words of our sages require no confirmation", which is a justification to all classes.

Thus, I think, it is sufficiently clear to everybody, how we see from ציצה and תפילין the close connection between love of God and love of our fellowmen.

(3) — ושמרתם לנפשותיכם כי לא ראיתם כל תמונה (דברים ד' ט"ו). "Take ye therefore good heed unto yourselves for ye saw no manner of Similitude" (Deutr. IV. 15). וראיתם את אחורי ופני לא יראו (שמות ל"ג כ"ג) And thou shalt see My backparts but My face shall not be seen" (Exod. XXXIII, 23). Many of our great philosophers and commentators of the holy writ agree that where it says of God אחורי, it means that part of His heavenly glory which He has manifested in this world, in His works. This is the only part of the knowledge of God accessible to us. We have no power nor right to study the glory of our heavenly Father, but of his creation, creatures

and actions. Unfortunately we meet a great many who like to acknowledge the benevolent hand of God only as long as they are happy, whealthy and successful in their undertakings, but he, who has thoroughly learnt to know human life, he, who has ever tried to study the creator of his glorious work of creation, who has reached a high standard of human development and perfection, will ask the question of Job: "Shall we את הטוב נקבל מאת האלהים ואת הרע לא נקבל? (איוב ב' י') receive the good at the hand of God and shall not receive evil" (Job II, 10.) Although there are many whom one or another arrangement in this world may displease, hurt or dissatisfy, yet they are only few, whereas the great majority at large derives unlimited Benefit of all that God has willed to give to this world or to do therewith, as it will be further on explained in Nr. 17.

There is still another way to explain this verse. Up to the present about sixty five elements are said to exist in creation, by composing and separating which, all discoveries in chemistry have been made hitherto and new ones will be made in future. Supposing that the word פני points to these very elements, the sentence could thus be explained. However much we will study the mystery of creation, we will only know these bare elements, but the way of creation, and the source of such an element, will always remain a mystery, which man will never be able to solve, nor will human knowledge ever be able to produce a new element, Whilst all the greatest capacites have and will have to devote the whole of their lives to discover these elements. Moses, in his time, was so far advanced in knowledge and wisdom, that he knew all of them, and made use of them in performing all the miracles dictated by God to Pharao in Egypt in presence of all the poeple. This would also explain the verse: ״ולא קם עוד נביא בישראל כמשה אשר ידעו ה' פנים אל פנים לכל האתת והמופתים i. e., (דברים ל"ד י' י"א) אשר שלחו ה' לעשית בארץ מצרים and yet there has been no prophet in Israel, like Moses, who had so great a knowledge of God that he knew the use of all elements in creation and the compositions thereof. But he knew still more, his knowledge was further advanced. He understood to use the elements in creation for producing such substances that will be useful for posterity, and to utilize them when necessary for the advantage of the world. Wishing to bring his beloved nation out of Egypt, their laud of bondage, and to make them receive the Thorah, his knowledge helped him to perform the greatest miracles. This has given foundation to Religion, that holy cord which unites the whole of the human race on earth. Without humanity, humane and moral principles all knowledge is of no value. as it says: ״סוף דבר הכל נשמע את אלהים ירא ואת מצותיו שמור כי זה כל האדם״ "Let us hear the conclusion of the whole matter, fear God and keep his commandments, for this is the whole man (Eccles. XII, 13.) Rifles, Guns and other firearms are of great importance and value, as they protect us before the wild beasts, dynamit is necessary and very useful to split great stones, to remove mountains, when laying a railroad, navigating a river etc. Nowa-days we find the very same inventions used in quite a different way and for quite another purpose. Rifles, guns and firearms in General, poeple, under the holy mask of politics, use, to take the life of innocent human beings on the field of battle, dynamit to kill thousands of their fellowmen in war. Such a use of those harmless chemical substances, surely was never intended by our Almighty Creator, and for this object, it would be far better, if knowledge would never have discovered them.

(4). — "ואהבת לרעך כמוך" "Love thy neighbour like thyself" (Levit. XIX, 18) This commandment bids us to love every one with whom we associate, who can be of use and advantage to us in any way whatsoever, of whom we can learn morals, manners etc. All they are entitled to our uninterested and sacrificing love, which we feel for our own selves. And since only he can truly love himself, who bases his life upon morality and humanity, who is aware of the high qualities, which place him higher above every other creature, such a man will always love his neighbour, without distinctions of race or creed.

This is the reason why the commandment of love to our fellowmen finishes with 'אני ה "I am God", an expression, which, though interpreted in many ways must always lead to the same conclusion.

It suould be mentioned, that all passages of the Holy Writ commanding us to love the stranger terminate with אני ה'.

(5). — ר' עקיבא אומר זה כלל גדול בתורה בן עזי אמר זה ספר תולדות האדם "Rabbi Akiba, referring to the verse of the above note says, it is the principal law in the Bible Ben Asai says it is the Book of Generations of mankind. What can be higher than the term of Rabbi Akiba, and why is Ben Asai induced to call it different? But Ben Asai, when giving his opinion, was thinking of the question: What have men been doing before they received the Thorah? What were those doing, who did not know yet of the holy Writ? Or what do the freethinkers do, who do not acknowledge the authority of the Holy Scripture, the necessity of religion? He came to the conclusion, that the feeling ot love to our fellowmen is a gift of God, implanted into the heart of every man born child and he explains this opinion by saying: "this is the book of human generations" i. e. This quality was with every human being at all times.

(6).—חביב האדם שנברא בצלם וכו' שנאמר בצלם אלהים
ברא את האדם (פרקי אבות ג' י"ח — עיין תוס' יו"ט שם גם עיין תוס'
יבמות י"א ותוס' ע"ז ג'.) "Beloved is a man for he was created in the image (of God) etc. for it says: In the image of God made he man" (Aboth III. 18.— Compare also Tosvoth Yomtov there and Tosvoth in Jebamoth 11 and Aboda Zara 3.) In all places above mentioned we find clearly explained by our Rabbis, that wherever it says: האדם, with a definite "ה" (ה הידיעה) it, means all men that fill the habitable globe, whilst the word אדם (without the definite ה) means only the Israelites. I just think to explain the meaning of our strictly orthodox and learned Rabbis this way. A human being only then deserves the name "man", when possessing humanity. But at the time of our great legislator all nations, except the Jews, had not yet learned to know the importance of humanity in life, nay some were even so wicked and corrupt that they offered their children up as sacrifices to their idols and were thus not worthy of the name אדם. Yet if amongst these wicked and evildoing masses there were men, who understood the importance of humanity and distinguished themselves, by moral principles, from others, such were regarded as equal to the Jews, no matter to what nation or creed they belonged, and wishing to point especially to such man, Moses used the word האדם with the definite article "the man". We also find that our Rabbis call such exceptionally good with the name "friend" רע חבר Just so we read: חסידי אומות העולם יש להם חלק לעולם הבא "The pious men of

every race have their share of future grace".

(7).—כי אתם ידעתם את נפש הגר. "For you know the spirit of a stranger (Exodus XXIII 9.) This great and important commandment is many times repeated in the Holy Scripture. But the Jews would never have been able to feel with the oppressed and persecuted, had they not themselves been subjected slavery and illtreatment in Egypt.

We all know, that one can never feel anything deep enough before he experiences it himself, and our Rabbis wisely teach us: אל תדין את חברך עד שתגיע למקומו "Judge not thy neighbour till thou art come into his place" (Aboth II, 5) i. e. never give your opinion upon anybody's position until you have duly experienced and investigated the same. Let me just give a parable to illustrate this: There was once a King, who was affraid, that his son and heir to the throne, being brought up in tenderness and surrounded with every kind of luxury, as Rulers' children usually are, will never be able, when taking the lead of Government, to listen to the cry of oppressed, to feel the position of the unfortunate of his subjects. He therefore decided to send him abroad and to limit his allowance gradually to a minimum When the son returned home he said: My father, there is nothing that can teach us so well as personal experience.

So would Jews never be able to acknowledge the pitiable position of the oppressed and persecuted, were they not subjected to slavery and illtreatment themselves in Egypt.

This very feeling caused by personal experience was one of the principal reasons why they were at once ready to accept the high morals of religion, prescribed by Moses in the name of God founded solely on humane and moral principles.

Our great Legislator went even so far, that he distinctly

told the Israelites, that even when they come to the holy land, the promised land, their inheritance, they have still not to forget that they are only sojourners there, and that they must thus all the more feel with the stranger. Therefore Moses says unto them in the name of God והארץ לא תמכר לצמיתות כי לי כל הארץ. "The land shall not כי גרים ותושבים אתם עמדי (ויקרא כ״ה כ״ג). be sold for ever, for all the land is Mine, for ye are only strangers and sojourners with me" (Levit. XXV. 23).

The Israelites have proved wonderfully obeying this Commandment, as we find that on a piece of land 33 by 20 miles they had as many as 153,600 strangers. This is confirmed in Chronicles II. 2, v. 6 (דברי הימים ב׳ ב׳ ו.).

(8).—Whenever the law speaks of "the stranger" גר it always adds "who dwells in your midst" הגר בתוככם — That the word גר did not refer to one who has newly embraced the Jewish faith is clearly seen in Deutr. XXVIII, 43, and Isaiah LVI. 1-9.

(9) — ולא תעשו מכל התועבות האלה האזרח והגר הגר בתוככם כי את כל התועבת האל עשו אנשי הארץ אשר לפניכם ותטמא הארץ "And ye shall not commit any of these abominations. neither any of your nation, nor any citizen and stranger that sojourneth amidst you. For all these abominations have the men of the land done, which were before you and the land became defiled. (Levit. XVIII. 26-27)

(10). — למען אשר יביאו בני ישראל את זבחיהם אשר הם זובחים על פני השדה והביאם לה׳ וכו׳ ולא יזבחו עוד את זבחיהם לשעירים. "In order that the children of Israel shall offer up their sacrifices, which they offer in the open field, and that they may bring them unto God etc. And they shall no more offer their sacrifices unto devils. Levit. XVII, 5-7.

In the explanation of these verses the Middrash agrees with the Rambam and adds an example in his commentary. (11).— השמרו לכם פן תשכחו את ברית ה' אלדהיכם אשר כרת "Take heed unto yourelves, lest you forget the covenant of the Lord your God, which He made with you, and make you a graven image the likeness of any thing, which the Lord thy God hath forbidden thee". (Deutr. IV. 23). It seems to me that Moses wished in this verse to guard his poeple against fanaticism of any kind. All commentaries experience great difficulty in wishing to explain the words אשר צוך ה' אלוהיך I think Moses meant to say: "Take heed that in studying the Commandments of God, you should not make them merely standing forms and formalities as the images are blindly worshipped without further moral principles. There were, for instance, many amongst the Jews who regarded מצות תפלין the commandment of frontlets and other commandments as a commaudment, to which they have blindly to obey, without taking the trouble to consider its moral connection with the duties of men and humanity, to which I referred above.

An illustration how fanaticism was brought about, will be seen in the following: Amongst the priests and clergy, who at all times were and still remain the spiritual guides of the Congregation we see three different classes. Some who really feel and acknowledge the high moral principles of humanity contained in the law, but who in order as to make them accessible to all mankind who shall abide by them, they had no other way but daggling the eyes of their congregants, others again did so out of the simple reason that they knew that to be a priest is a good position and pays well. But there were also such, especially in later days, who after having seen and heard the details related of the previous two classes, took the commandment simply as a fanaticism and treated it as such. To this, I think, it is due, that we meet now-a-days fanaticism so often not only with the Jews, but in every creed. But in face of this, already the prophets, knowing that the true basis of every commandment is only morality and humanity, strongly protested against blind obedience and fanaticism, trying to press upon and preach only of true religion, bare of any fanatical ingredient and based solely upon our moral conduct and human feelings. (Isaiah X, 2 and the whole chapter LVIII etc.)

(12)—Think not that I am come to destroy the law or the prophets; I am not come to destroy but to fulfill. Whosoever therefore shall break one of these least commandments, and shall teach men so he shall be called the least in the Kingdom of Heaven. (St. Mathew VI 17. 19.)

The passages quoted above from the New Testament, will show, that Christ did not intend to give his followers a new creed, but he showed the Pharisees a way of making religion more comprehensible to mankind in developing its moral and human principles in a popular way to his disciples, who all were offsprings of the Jewish race, in order as to induce all nations of the habitable globe to acknowledge the unity of God and the necessity of love, sincere love, not only towards our friends but even towards our enemies.

Religiously speaking we can only hate and despise a man who is of corrupt and immoral habits, and as such a man not only is hated by others, but he also feels love for nobody, he is called "שנא„ (enemy i. e. one who hateth thee). But at the same time, with reference to such enemies of ours, we are command-

כי תפגע שור איבך או חמרו תועה השב תשיבנו לו. ed by Moses:
כי תראה חמור שנאך רבץ תחת משאו וחדלת מעזוב לו — עזב תעזוב עמו.
(שמות כ"ג ד' ה') 'If thou meetest thy enemy's ox or ass erring thou shalt surely return it unto him. If thou seest the ass of thy foe lying beneath his burden and thou willst not help him; thou must surely help him. (Exodus XXIII 4, 5.

Our sages say: אהב לפרק ושנא לטעון שנא קדם (ב"מ ל"ב ומסח' קיינ') When having to unload the cargo of a friend and to take the enemy's cargo, we must give the preference to the enemy, doing his first.

תוספות explains there, that as an enmity because of corrupt character always entails another enmity, because of personal interest, we can never be able to weigh, which of the two is mightier, and therefore we must serve our enemy first. This has been afterwards repeated in the new Testament, where to explain it distinctly it says: "But I say unto you, love your enemies, bless them that course you, do good to them that hate you, and pray for them which despitefully use you and prosecute you etc. For He maketh His sun rise on the evil and on thn good and sendeth rain on the just and on the unjust. (St. Mathew V. 44, 45).

These high moral principles have been accepted and acknowledged by many good thinking poeple, who were ready to sacrifice even their lives for their true und strict observance. But in course of time, owing to the fanaticism of the clergy, which gradually predominated in the manner aforesaid, their principles were so misinterpreted, that the fanatics became tyrants and thousands were brutally slaughtered, because they stuck to the very principles, which Christ himself preached. This was the origin of the great historical event, called the "Spanish Inquisition".

Many Christians hate Jews because their forefathers have killed Christ. If we will carefully study the New Testament and secular history of the beginning of the christian era, we will easily find, that both, the sentence and crucification of the Founder of Christianity were, but a conspiracy of Pilate and Herod, who were both not of Jewish descent. Jews have even always been against them. But as it was in their own interest to gain the favour of the government and the people, they have done their cruel deeds through the priests, who, in their turn found it then very practical, and were even compelled to seek the sympathy of the rulers, because they appointed them. Moreover we find it many times mentioned in the New Testament that the Herodians were great enemies of Christ and tried to interfere on every occasion acting against Christ and his followers. Compare: Mathew XXII. 16; Mark III. 6; VI. 14; VIII. 15; XII. 14; Luc. VI. 7; XXIII, 7 etc.) In St. John XVIII, 37, we read: "Pilate therefore said unto him: "Art thou a King"? he answered "thou sayest I am a King".

If we follow the contents of the whole chapter, we find that Pilate fully believed Christ was King and wished him punished as an impostor, but Christ never gave a plain and straight answer to his questions. Moreover Pilate had reason to fear that Christ will proclaim himself a King. In Luc. XXIII. 11 we see that Herod and his elders laughed at Christ and mocked him, and we will see in onother chapter, when Pilate pleads his cause before the people, he tries also to defend Herod and to take his part. Now what reason had Pilate to defend Herod, who mocked Christ? If Pilate again believed Christ, why did he assault when he sent him away? Why did he allow his soldiers to illtreat Christ? It was not only Christ whom Herod tried to get rid of, He also put to death Zaducees Pharisees even Members of the Sanhedrin and others.

As a proof that the Jews were innocent on that sentence, we can see, that Rabbi Gamliel, who, when the Apostles were brought up for sentence before the Sanhedrin, exclaimed: "By cruel law, you will not destroy this, if it is the will of God". (Acts V, 34), We also read in St. John (XVIII, 31) that when Pilate brought Christ for sentence before the Jews, they said: "It is not lawful for us to put any man to death."

But, after all, if we should even suppose for a moment that more than 1800 years ago, some ancestors of the present Jews were concerned in Christ's crucifixion, what of it? May we blame their posterity now after so many centuries? Dit not Jeremiah say: "לא יאמרו עוד אבות אכלו בסר ושני בנים תיקהנה?" "They will no more say, Fathers have eaten unripe fruit and the sons' teeth shall become hollow" (Jeremiah XYXI, 29) Did not Ezekiel say "בן לא ישא בעון אב ונפש החטאת היא תמות" "The son shall not bear the father's sin, and the person that sinneth shall die? (Ezekiel XXXI 18). All that referreed to the time when the world will be far enough advanced in humanity. Now, is it possible, and is it not a shame, if it be a fact, that in the XIX century, the century of civilisation, the world should still be so far back as to make the thousandth generation suffer for a nearly two thousandth years old sin of their ancestors? If we think to open the books of history and go to account, every nation beginning from the Greeks and finishing with the most civilised deserves persecution. The Greeks treacherously killed Socrates and every nation has to memorate plenty of cruel inhuman and atrocious deeds in their history. Happily, time makes us forget, but we must forget all, and if we remember one, why not think of the others?

Just speaking of the verse ולא יאמרו עוד אבות אכלו בסר ושני בנים תקהנה in Jeremiah, I remind myself, that in the next verse, where it says: "And I shall make a new covenant with the House of Israel and the House of Judah". The Missionaries wish to mean the teaching of the New Testament as the new covenant. But, since a new covenant can only be made when sins of fathers will not be visited on their offsprings, how can they wish those to believe their teaching, upon whom they constantly throw the guilt of their ancestors? Jeremiah further says: "ולא ילמדו עוד איש את אחיו ואיש את רעהו לאמר דעו את ה' כי כולם ידעו אותי למקטנם ועד גדולים" "And they will no more teach each one his brother and each one his friend saying: Know ye the Lord, for all will know Me from the least of them, unto the greatest of them". Yes, when all will know God and there will be no more want of teachers then will the possibility of a new covenant be a fact, but now, when each one does not believe the theory of his neighbour, when each one fights for the truth of an idea opposed to by his friend, when the truth, the absolute truth, acknowledged by the whole human race, is still a dark mystery, can we speak of a new covenant? Can we say that the time, that blessed time of perfect knowledge and a new covenant has already approached? that the new covenant has already been made?

I should therefore ask those generous, liberal and benevolent men, who, true to their creed, support Missions, that they should take great care, to make these Institutions a school and home where inmates should be kept to learn morals and rules of true humanity, not as these institutions are now a stock-exchange for creeds, for the purchase of souls, for getting Jews who have a too limited knowledge of their faith to embrace Christianity for a promise, and apromise only of monetary reward. We know that the Jews were and are still now the teachers of morals and humanity to all the universe. Surely they do not want to be taught. But there are many of other creeds, who require and badly require such teaching. Let them be taught, let these institutions be open to such destitute and ignorant poeple, and I am sure, the church will reap much more Benefit, than by bargaining Jewish souls, dear, nay, too dear bargains for the present civilized XIX Century.

Every creed ought to strive to propagate humanity amidst its own followers, leaving other creeds to do the same for themselves. This will be the only means for promoting universal peace and happiness, as will be seen from the letter of the great russian philosopher W. Solovieoff on page 9 of this pamphlet and in the New Testament from St. Matthew XXII v. 36—40 according to which this is one principal destination in our earthly life.

(13).—The two letters, written by the late Emperor Frederic III to the Reichskanzler Bismarck "the iron prince" will remain a living memorial to this everlamented humane Ruler. The Emperor therein complained, that owing to their insufficient development in science and study, the german people are unable to value the merits of true humanity.

It makes one's heart rejoice, seeing the present young

Emperor William II. walking in the footsteps of his never to be forgotten father, of his royal mother, and of his beloved grandmother Her Most Gracious Majesty Victoria Queen of Gt. Britain, Empress of India. Only lately he has expressed himself, after the style of his father's enlightened views, and I hope, that, young and vigorous as he is, he will serve as a good example to other european states.

Speaking about the German Emperor, I may perhaps be allowed to offer a humble suggestion. According to my idea the peace and prosperity that the european nations now enjoy depend entirely on Emperor William II., and the first step towards disarmement and general peace, would be that Germany and France shall co-operate together, and I hope, that France will compensate Germany with such a sum, that Germany will be satisfied with such an exchange.

(14)—לא בחיל ולא בכח כי אם ברוחי אמר ה' צבאורת•
(Zechariah) IV. 6.

(15)—כי היא חכמתכם ובינתכם לעיני העמים• (Deutr. 4, 6.)

(17.)—These three oaths are also mentioned in the Talmud (Kesuboth כתובות קי״ג)

From all that has been said about the last of the three oaths and Jacob's forgetfulness, when desirous of revealing the Milenium to his sons, we must understand: 1) that we mortals must never allow ourselves to think of plans for an end of all things and for the approach of the Milenium, for it is not in human power to bring about this happy period. We must arm ourselves with tolerance and patiently await the time when all mankind will be so far advanced as to properly understand each other, to have the same views, equal ideas and to arrive at the same conclusions. Then, in those happy days, all will be understood by human race alike. 2) We can impossibly think, that the world will be in time so far advanced, that we will see but good and not meet with evil. This is absolutely unimaginable and ridiculous.

For, as it is repeatedly proved in this pamphlet, we can only know what is good, if we see the evil, we can only distinguish the perfect, if we see the imperfect at the side of it, and, were there no evil, we could never think of good, as when there is no nice, we cannot imagine the ugly, without light we would never be able to concevie and imagine the dark. Just because we know that something is wrong we avail ourselves of the opportunity to choose the better. Just because we know of something nice, we endeavour to avoid the ugly; because we know tedious and monotonous ways, we will try to find that which is pleasant and agreeable. Thus, if we have the bad, the wrong, the ugly and the unpleasant, we find ample scope to improve our fancy, taste and imagination, our thoughts, ways and actions, and avoiding carefully that which opposes our desire, we will do our utmost to reach always the better, to gain perfection and pleasure at the same time.

It is the same with science and its offspring inventions. Whatever is made by a skillful hand, is being improved by others and the longer we will live, the more, inventions of the present day will gain in improvement.

Fully conscious of this we should never say that, because we have chosen some object or some plan or way, it is the very best. In whatever we do we cannot, as mortals, be so careful as to give others no opportunity to improve our work. We see that in a great many of our modern inventions, as

Railway, Gaslight etc. only the advantageous points were considered by the inventors, who, of course, could by no means foresee, that the slightest oversight, a trifling mistake in use, will do great harm. And, speaking of inventions at large, we must say, that, whilst they do a great deal of good, they will do much more harm, if we would for one moment abandon the greatest care, which is needed, whilst making use of such inventions. And it must be so; for human mind, just because it is human, is absolutely unable to foresee all that may arise in consequence of such or other use of our inventions, and, most perfect as it may be in course of time, human mind will never be able to remove all disadvantages of anything it invents with the best of intentions for the use of posterity.

We will thus find nothing unconditionally perfect in this world, and it would be as ridiculous to think of something absolutely good, absolutely right, perfect, nice or pleasant, as it is impossible to find something absolutely bad, wrong, imperfect or ugly, as it is expressed in the words: "מפי עליון לא תצא הרעות והטוב" — "Out of the Most High proceedeth not the evil and the good" (Lament III 38.) i. e. the absolutely evil and the unconditionally good.

Some thing will only appear bad and unpractical for a moment, but we will soon find, on careful consideration, that its goodness or practicability will depend on our care, we use it with, and were a certain useless or even noxious invention used with due care on our part, we will very soon find its practicability and use.

Just as it is with inventions it is with thoughts, opinions and ideas.

For instance, if we find hundreds of workingmen complaining, that owing to the fact that a certain trade having become overcrowded in course of time, they are not able to earn half as much as they used in days gone by, — such a state, we would say, is deplorable. But if we will consider, that owing to a greater number of people having taken to a certain trade, the articles this trade produces, have become much cheaper, easier accessible to the poorer class, that the want of such articles has gone so far as to give employment to so many hundreds of peoenle, we will find the advantage of it. It is very bad, if a place is visited by a contagious disease, and at such times medical advice being needed everywhere, the medical men at disposal will never satisfy the wants of the population. The consequences of this are, that hundreds must fall victims to the desease, because they were not attended to. But if we would endeavour to have always a sufficient number of Doctors, chemists and inventors, why, we would easily be able not only to attend to all our patients, not only to quench the malady, but we would have such means discovered as to prevent the ingress of the morbid disease and who knows not that: "prevention is better than cure".

I therefore think, that the monies used by the world now for the produce of fire arms, war materials and monuments, which besides that do no good, cause great harm to the world at large, if those monies, I say, would be used for the support of those, who devote themselves to study and science, we would feel no lack of good medical men, thorough chemists and very clever inventors in the moment of need.

We hear very often people complain of poverty, day by day, nay hour by hour, we see heartrending proofs of need.

want and misery. But this state of things must necessarily exist in the world, or else we would know nothing of pity, of commiseration, of charity and Benevolence. There would be no love of one man to another. Moses was therefore justified by saying unto his people in the name of God: כי לא יחדל אביון מקרב הארץ "For the poor shall never cease out of the land" [Deutr. XV, 11.] (Relying on this Verse of the Bible the Rabbi Samuel found his theory of אין בן ימות עולם הזה לימות המשיח אלא שיעבוד מלכיות בלבד) [v. page VIII, 15.] We find a Medrash in Exodus XXXI, where in verse 7 of Psalm 61 is referred to ישב עולם לפני אלדים חסד ואמת מן ינצרוהו "He shall abide before God for ever mercy and truth may preserve him.

Following the Hebrew text and explaining this verse the Medrash tells us: David asked of God "why the world is not entirely perfect, why are all men not equally gifted materially and morally"? and received the reply: "If the world will be all perfect and good, without any difference, who will exercise benevolence and deeds of charity, mercy and kindness? And no human being, be he whoever he is, can possibly exist without being dependent on his fellowmen.

A Kotzebue in his "Ausbruch der Verzweiflung" says:
„Kaum geboren findet schon
„Jedes Huhn sein bischen Futter;
„Kaum geboren, hüpft schon
„Jedes Huhn um seine Mutter;
„Nur der Mensch, ein Gabelthier
„Kann sich keinen Schritt entfernen,
„Und der Schöpfung stolze Zier,
Muss erst geh'n und essen lernen.
Whilst nearly every animal, from its very infancy can

and does try for its own maintenance, a human being, when born, must for long years be dependent on the care of his parents in every little trifle, and when he reaches manhood, he still cannot call himself independent of his fellow citizen, both in material and moral way. And as one man can only improve, being influenced by another, so can the whole world, consisting of human beings, reckon only upon advance, if every individual does endeavour to exercise its whole influence upon another.

This is the law of nature and it can impossibly be different. For if it were to the contrary, viz. if human beings could exist independent of each other and every one for himself, the world would come not one step forward and men would be nothing more than cattle.

An illustration of this true idea we will find in the philosophical and allegorical teachings of our Rabbis: Rabbi Elieser ben Pedos, so says the Talmud, once complained before the Almighty of his extreme poverty. He received the following reply: ניחא לך דאחרבה לעלמא והדר אבריה ואפשר דמברירת בשעתא דמזוני, אמרה קמיה רבוניה דעלמא כולי דהאי ואפשר "Wilt thou be satisfied if I overthrow the universe, and then perhaps, thou mayest be created in a time of plenty. (Taanith III.)

Two questions crop up unwillingly, when reading this description. 1.) Rabbi Elieser ben Pedos was very poor, did he, that pious and tolerant Rabbi, really complain about his poverty to the Almighty himself? 2.) If he did, would the eternal answer him "perhaps", would he speak of a probability? to creat a new world in which he, Rabbi Elieser, may be, will feel himself more happy?

These two questions, important as they seem, will be easily

— 57 —

solved and answered, if we follow my above theory. Rabbi Elieser ben Pedos was at the verge of poverty need and starvation. Pious as he was, he armed himself with as much perseverance and constancy as he possibly could and many a time went into counsel with his heart, soul and mind, his חל״ק אלה ממעל "by a part from on high". He could not comprehend, why need and misery is existing at all? and why Providence has willed it that he, the good and pious shall tremendously suffer, whilst some wicked and careless are happy and wealthy? רשע וטוב׳לו צדיק ורע לו And what did he find? When his experience in human nature was so far advanced, that he knew well, what position men occupy in this world, he became aware of the great fact, that the world can by no means be arranged different to what it is now. If we had only good and perfect men in this world, we would see no evil in opposition to it, thus we would not recognise the good from the bad, losing the choice between the good and evil —בחירה— unable to do the right and avoid the wrong.

Again, if we would see the world arranged so that all righteous men should be affluent and happy and all wicked men miserable, who would like to be wicked? Would they not all be good, perfect and just? (We often see that a man does wrong notwithstanding that he is aware of the severe punishment awaiting him by law. We can accout for it either because he sees that if even he is righteous, he is bad off or because he thinks the authorities will not notice his wrongs. But if Providence would have rewarded the good and punished the wicked, would one be so stupid to do wrong?) Thus we would only witness the good, the right, the perfect and see no trace of evil and injustice, but in this way we could never form an opinion about the evil, we would never know, what to do and what to avoid, and as the "good" is precious only because there is "evil", we would never know how to value the good and avoid the bad. Such were the thoughts of our pious Rabbi when he considered his position. And it was then that he heard the reply of his spirit within, of his חלק אלה ממעל to the effect, that for the worlds own benefit and advantage, things must remain as they are, and that hence the world will learn to recognise the great difference between good and evil, and always have an open way for moral improvement.

This is also the reason why as the Thalmud describes there Rabbi Elieser was then seen in a fit, laughing and crying alternatively and a spark of fire flashed across his face, this spark indicating the standard of perfection he had reached, understanding, that if the world were not managed by providence as wisely as it is, men would be no more than cattle. And what human being would allow even to be only compared with cattle? Surely no one; and in order as to fulfill the duty of man — every one tries to become perfect and wise. But we find in Eccles. (קהלת א' י"ח) ברב חכמה רב כעס "The more wisdom the more wrath". True, the wiser we get, the more do we feel, how much we neglect our duties. But though we are never satisfied with the standard of wisdom we reach, yet we would never change with those who stand lower than we do. We may often even envy them, think them happier, but we will not play their part. Although we may sometimes see the wise man envying a fool, who is much more satisfied with his life, than he ever will be, who has all he wants and wishes no better—yet he will never change with the fool. How often does a freethinker believe the fanaticist to be more happy than himself, more content with the course of his moral life yet he will never think of parting with his opinions and adopting fanaticism.

Let us then adopt as the best of all the advice of Ecclesiastes (קהלת ג' י"ח) אין טוב בם כי אם לשמוח ולעשות טוב בחייו "There is nothing better than to rejoice one's life and to do good."

We can, basing on this theory easily explain the dispute which existed between Beth-Shamai and Beth-Hillel on the subject „טוב שלא נברא משנברא ועכשיו כשנבוא יפשפש במעשיו" (עירובין י"ג), on which they could not agree for full 2 years and a half. Our Rabbis say in Erubim 13. "It is better for man not to be created than to be created, but if he is once created let him see that all his actions should be perfect, just and useful to himself and of benefit to the world at large.

This explanation also expresses the difference between public opinion and that of the socialists, who think that if work and wages, capital and labour, pleasures and enjoyments will be equally divided, all will be happy and satisfied, one will love his fellowman and poverty will ultimately cease. As we have shown above, this is against law of nature and can never become a reality.

Looking upon the different trades people are devoting their lives to, we will find amongst them a large number, which endangering the lives of those, who cultivate them on the other hand are of the greatest use and benefit to the world at large. We will also find such callings, which people would have quite neglected, were it not for the sake of earning their scanty living, for which they are bound to try. Would for instance a coal, salt, gold or silver miner undertakes to go down into these mines for the purpose of finding one of these articles, an act connected with the risk of his life at any moment, if he had not the profit in view which he realizes by performing so audacious and dangerous a task. Would he, we ask, be ready to put his life, the dearest treasure of his own and his family at stake, if he were not prompted by need, by poverty or by the desire of earning a livelihood? And yet all the articles such miners find are of the utmost importance to the world and whilst theym ay entail the risk and sometimes loss of human life, on the other hand they are of enormous benefit to the world at large. the unconditional companions in our daily life, they give us health, pleasure and comfort.

Besides those who make a calling their own as a means of livelihood, there are others, who indulge in a trade in order to increase their wealth, their capital. Their only wish is to have more than a neighbour has.

To do this may be a very wrong motive, but if we leave reasons aside for a moment, we must admit that whatever such people do, be it for one reason or another is always useful to the world at large. Nay even the bad qualities, they are possessed of, are of great benefit, provided of course, such bad qualities are not indulged in to excess, so that they might hurt or interfere with our fellowman's rights and privileges, or limit his moral freedom.

Envy, money, honour etc. are then often the principal reasons, why one devotes himself to one trade or branch of cience, the other to another and so it must be. For should this desire die away, as the Socialists argue, we will always meet with revolutions, dissatisfaction, we will hear of wars over and over again. The world will and can never be satisfied entirely!

We see in our daily life, that father and son or two brothers, brought up in the same way, trained by one master entirely differ in their opinions, views and ideas, whilst one approves of something the other blames it, and prefers to take quite a different view of the subject. How can we than expect a whole world to agree?

After all that has been above said we will be well able to easily explain the allegorical meaning of the history about the man and עץ הדעת the tree of knowledge of which we are told in Genesis, the Book of creation. On speaking of the עץ הדעת the Rambam רמב"ם tells us, that he was asked the question: If Adam committed a sin by transgressing the command of God, why is it, that instead of being punished by degradation, he was promoted to a higher standard of progress?

Following the explanation given below this question will easily be answered.

It is to be regretted, and yet it is a fact, that there were, are and that there will at all times be such individuals and even whole nations or provinces, who either by their own religious fanaticism or by that of their rulers, kings, clergymen or spiritual guides disregard and despise education, as to their opinion disadvantageous to the world or weakening the strength and power of religion. History tells us that in the middle ages hundreds of people were barbarously put to death in certain countries in the name of religion or rather religious fanaticism for the only reason that they sought for knowledge. It is natural that such nations will hate and ridicule every new discovery every invention, as for instance they say that the Chinese were overcome with an immense fright, seeing a miniature locomotive-engine, which their emperor ordered to be made for his private use. As every advance in knowledge and science was regarded by such people a sin, in the name of God and religion, Moses has been forced to call those advanced men, who, in fact, wished to promote progress, but whose influence was regarded by the religious fanatic guides as unhealthy and poisonous to their subject "serpents" who beguiled mankind to do what they were forbidden. The whole passage about Eve, the serpent and man in relation to the tree of knowledge, tends to show the beginning of development of human mind, the first step of man towards the knowledge of good and evil, a sin in the eyes of people and in face of religion, therefore as dangerous and poisonous as a serpent, but in fact, in reality the most evident mark of progress. That it is so, we can see from the words כי ביום אכלכם ממנו ונפקחו עיניכם והייתם כאלהים יודע טוב ורע (בראשית ג' ה') "For on the day ye eat therefrom your eyes will be opened and ye will become as gods knowing good and evil". (Gen. III 5.) And indeed, as soon as man had tasted the fruit of the tree of knowledge, his first step towards advance was made, as we read afterwards in v. 22 of the same chapter (שם ג' כ"ב) הן האדם היה כאחד ממנו לדעת טוב ורע "Behold the man became as one of us in knowledge of" good and evil" thus giving us to understand that the knowledge of the difference between good and evil constitutes one of the points of similarity of likeness of man unto his Maker

But the word אלהים does not only apply to the Almighty alone, it also signifies „judges, rulers" etc. as we find אלהים לא תקלל (שמות כ"ב כ"ח) "Thou shalt not revile judges" (Exodus XXII. 28.) עד האלהים יבא דבר שניהם (שם כ"ב ה') "The cause of both parties shall come before the judges" (ibid XXII. 8.) The learned Rambam fully agrees with this, and in his "Moreh Nebochim" Chapt. 2, he brings the same verse and refers to the Thargum, where אלהים is translated by רברביה and means kings, judges etc. (עיין מורה נבוכים חיא פיב) (According to this opinion of the Rambam, whereas אלהים means also kings, judges and spiritual guides, we may explain the verse: ויראו בני אלהים את בנות האדם כי טובות הנה ויקחו להם נשים מכל אשר בחרו (שם ו' ב') "And the sons of the superiors saw the daughters of men, that they were nice looking and they took wifes unto themselves whichever they choose" (ibid VI. 2.) The children of the highest civil and ecclesiastical authorities were morally so far advanced that they choose their wifes not as hitherto from amidst their equals, family or relatives, but from amongst the people, whilst the people themselves reckoned this as a sin, as we can see in the next verses and in the Thalmud.) With regard to יהוה there is an important passage in the "Zohar" וזהר דק' in the explanation of the verse שלש פעמים בשנה יראה כל זכורך. — (Moreh Nebuchim I. 65, wherever the words "saying" or "speaking" is mentioned in connection with God it indicates only a desire.)

We can therefore come to the conclusion that not only God, but also Kings, Judges and spiritual guides of the people (their clergy) have forbidden their congregants at different times in the past to stretch out a hand for the tree of knowledge

עץ הדעת — But in the long run they could not always prevent it, and people's mind had to break the yoke of submission. They had to act against the command of their superiors, and so they began to advance and to grasp gradually more and more from the fruits of the עץ הדעת, of moral progress.

But, as soon as they had tasted the sweet fruits of progress, another tree presented itself to their sight, it was the עץ החיים "the tree of life" that tree of which it is said, that whoever tastes it's fruits וחי לעולם "and he will live for ever". But "עולם„ does not always mean "for ever" eternity, it means also unlimited, pleasant, free, as we find of a servant who loves his master, it says ועבדו לעולם, whereupon the Thalmud says it means till the יובל the jubilee year.

People, as we said above, had already a notion of progress they knew the taste of its sweet fruits and felt now a desire for a pleasant and agreeable life. On the other hand the rulers and clergy of the people, in forcibly keeping them back from longing after knowledge and wisdom, eo ipso prevented them from dreaming even of a free and peaceful life.

Having seen how their command was being transgressed and disregarded, they feared, that they will lose their influence with their subjects and congregants and thought הן האדם היה באחד ממנו "behold man has become as one of us", In order as to prevent this, they sought for a plan, if they could no more prevent the people from grasping the fruit of the tree of knowledge, to at least do all in their power to barricade the way of the tree of happy life. In order as to secure the success of their endeavours the clergy and rulers placed two sentries before the way leading to the tree of life, the כרובים the symbol of religion, the mysterious religious fanaticism passing into bigotry and superstition, the art of inventing new creeds, each one hating and despising the other and the להט דחרב דמתהפכת "the flaming sword that revolveth", the politics and political wars. Both these sentries have shut up the way and "guarded the tree of life" as the Bible says. Religious fanaticism on one hand taught the people to follow the superstitious ideas of their clergy and rulers to hate every other creed but their own, and made life very miserable and unhappy. The other, the so called "politics" had quite the same effect. Wars, fights and battles by reason of envy and other paltry circumstances, cause only great harm to the people and, ipso facto, prevent a happy and peaceful life.

Unfortunately within the last decades the number of obstacles to progress and happiness has increased by a third addition, another enemy of all that is good and useful, an offspring of the two former. the so called "religious and political press". This new enemy has shown himself in the shape of newspapers, conveying to the people the mind and intention of their rulers and priests, working either in a religious or in a political direction has no pure, neutral uninterested tendency, and whilst it defends the interests of one creed or political party, it condemns the affairs and principles of another. It is only too evident, how disadvantageous and dangerous this enemy is and that it must prevent people from finding the good or even from looking for it at all.

Having thus transgressed the command of their superiors and plucked off the fruit of the tree of knowledge, all who have participated in this transgression were cursed. So tells us the Scripture further. We will investigate these curses and endeavour to show that they were intended to show to the human race, that where "good" has come into existence, "evil" rose immediately in opposition to it, in other words, that good and evil are twins born at the same moment and bred by one another, and that these curses on the whole promoted the amelioration of the state of human race, benefitted the world at large·

First came the serpent, i. e. those who being themselves far advanced in education and science, trying to spread light of wisdom in the world, were regarded as poisonous as a "serpent" by the untaught majority and their spiritual guides. They were doomed to be in their position worse off than cattle, for cattle have no feeling for their lot, they bear it instinctively and patiently and are satisfied, whilst men of science, the more they study, the more they deplore their state and position, as we read in proverbs (משלי) יוסיף דעת יוסיף מכאוב "the more knowledge the more woe" They were further cursed to be always in trouble for their daily bread, as we often see that most learned men are in a very pressed, nay sometimes destitute financial position, לא לחכמים לחם "the wise have no bread". That their food be unto them like dust i. e. that they may never enjoy their hard but scanty earnings with comfort and satisfaction, but always be in trouble about their necessaries of life. That enmity shall exist between them and their fellowmen, which shall continue between the offsprings of both, a cruel and unremitting hatred. That the general public despise them "first" (beginning ראש) laughing at and ridiculing their best plans, thoughts and ideas, but, that after all, they prove victorious at the "end" (heel, end, עקב) and disregard those who scorned their wise and healthy ideas. (Gen. III., 14-15) Next came the woman.

If we follow Scripture we will find that the human race coming into life knew absolutely nothing of moral or material, mental or bodily want, as we read ויהיו שניהם ערומים האדם ואשתו ולא יתבוששו (בראשית ב' כ"ח) "They were both naked, the man and his wife and were not ashamed" (Genesis II, 25). They did not care at all about their nakedness. But immediately after having tasted of the fruit of the tree of knowledge we find a great change (שם ג' ז') ותפקחנה עיני שניהם וידעו כי ערומים הם "And the eyes of both were opened and they knew that they were naked (ibid III. 7.)

Curious enough, their nakedness, which did not concern them before, was the very condition which called forth their attention and awakened them to better their condition both morally and materially. Then only it came to pass that they thought of means for covering their nakedness, in order as to prevent the increase of man's animal-feelings, which, when they were naked, could only encourage frivolity and immorality. But to remove this inclination of man to immorality and corruption was not the work of days, or years, it took centuries, nay it is in some nations still struggling for its abolition. Why, the services offered in later days, in and long after Bible times, by the non-jewish population to their gods, were still full with apalling scenes of cruelty and moral corruption. The way people served the Baal-Peor and the other gods was but a succession of immoral and evil acts of horror, (we find therefore in the Bible the expression (במדבר ט"ו ל"ט) אשר אתם זונים אחריהם Comp. Numb. XV. 39 and Deutr. XXXI. 16, etc. The mythology of the Greeks and Romans contains not less abominable and horrible descriptions of services. Thus, in course of time, men began to feel, how injurious their ways are to themselves and the world at large, they did their first step to the better. So far for the moral advantage of covering the body of man. Its material advantages are just as great The necessity of something in the shape of clothing (מלבוש) to protect us from rain, cold heat and other changes of the air gave rise to shape, taste, fancy and became the mother of manufacture, trade and commerce, without which the world could not possibly exist. As it were, those people who were the first to feel the necessity of a means for putting a stop to the increase of demoralization, those people, who, though the then wisest of men, were regarded as serpents by their less instructed fellowmen, did their best to approach that class of human beings, which was both morally and materially the initiative to corruption, that class most sensitive towards vanity, fancy and beauty, most susceptible to religious fanaticism *"the woman"*.

At a glance we will see that whilst originally human kind was forbidden *to eat* of the fruit of the tree of knowledge, the woman answered the serpent, who tried to beguile and influence her "that they were bid not even *to touch it*", whereupon the Thalmud remarks, that the serpent pushed the woman on to the tree of knowledge, thus showing her, that the touch of the tree of knowledge entails no evil consequences. And the serpent succeeded to beguile the woman, who outstretched her hand and tasted the sweet fruit. But punishment came very soon after. The spiritual guides pronounced their curse upon her. They put it into her mind, that because she has transgressed their command and longed for knowledge her delivery and conception will be connected with great pains.

Such teachings repeat themselves very often in the history

of mankind, and even now at the end of the XIX century of civilzation, we will come across the fact, that a fanatical clergyman will make his superstitious congregants believe, that a sudden accident, that visited them, a misfortune which has come about unexpectedly is the consequence of their sins, the punishment for their transgressions.

They further made a very good step forward, which, however, not properly understood by the majority, was regarded, as all other benefits derived from science, as a curse. They took the chie motive of corruption, out of the power of the woman as it says (שם) ואל אישך תשוקתך והוא ימשול בך "And unto thy husband shall be thy desire, but he shall rule over thee" (ibid) i. e. that a woman shall in all her wishes, physical and mental, material as well as moral, be subdued to her husband, who shall rule over the desires of her heart, who is to supervise her inclinations, and as the case may be, allow o r disallow them. How great the power of man over the heart of the woman and her inclinations has become in course of time, is sufficiently proved by the commands given by Moses to his people in the name of God in Numbers Chapter XLII. (במדבר מ״ב)

The man because he has tasted the fruits of the tree of knowledge has also been cursed like unto the "serpent" the cause of his moral gain and progress. He was told, that this desire for "the forbidden fruit, for knowledge", brought about by the influence of his well persuaded companion of life "the woman" will make him feel that he must work with the sweat of his brow for his daily bread, that the world wiil never appreciate his endeavours It put into his mind the words spoken centuries

later by Fredrick v. Schiller, the unforgotten German poet:
„Wer nie sein Brod in Thraenen ass.
„Wer nie auf seinem Bette weinend sass,
„der kennt euch nicht, ihr himmlischen Maechte".
„Who never eat his bread in tears,
„Who never weeping spent his nights,
„Who in search of good not evil fears,
„He know ye not, ye Heaven's mights".

Whilst he will have to struggle bitterly for his existence plenty of thorns and thistles will meet him, plenty of obstacles will be found on his way. Every thing he will invent, every thing he may discover will meet with mockery and ridicule, and once he started to gain knowledge, he will feel that there w ll be no end to his endeavours, once he began to study and learn. he will always find that the end of knowledge is the true conviction that we know nothing. He will understand hat on his banner of which he "the king in creation" boasts the words will be written "For thou art dust and unto dust thou wilt return". Whatever he will think good, others will find bad, whatever seems to him healthy. nice and useful, will be regarded by others as noxious, ugly and useless, the more he will seek "the good" the more will he find "the evil". However perfect his idea may be, there will always be others, who know better and thus the latest ages will bear only — infant sages. (Comp. Genesis II.) This passage then finishes up with the words ויעש ה' אלהים לאדם ויאשתו כתנות עור וילבישם "And the the Lord God made unto Adam and his wife garments of skin and clothed them (ibid).

The Thalmud tells of Rabbi Meir, that in his copy of the Torah or after his style (בתורתו של רבי מאיר) עור was spelt with an א meaning "light". This would tell us, that he who understands the Torah from a scientific point of view, in a philosophical light, as Rabbi Meir, without ingredients of superstition and fanaticism, will clearly see that these curses brought with them a covering of true light, unmingled purity and holiness upon the world, whilst at the same time unto the fanaticist or passionate student, these curses will be a garment of skins tending to harden him against and prevent every influence of education and wisdom.

The theory of the curse o human race so explained will also disprove the system propagated by the modern socialists who wishing for equality of all mankind would only desire to reduce them to their very primitive state, i. e. that all go about naked. For if we will only begin to speak of clothing we will at once meet with shape, colour, fancy etc., which will satisfy one and dissatisfy another producing the results quoted above. We have sufficiently illustrated in the foregoing pages, how injurious nakedness is to man bodily and morally and will without further comments, see now how ridiculous their theory becomes.

Just as Moses thought it necessary to prescribe the sacrifices as a command of God in order to bring his people to the standard that they may acknowledge the absolute necessity of love of God and love of man, as we explained above, so has he been obliged to reproduce the כרובים Cherubim in an allegorical way, meaning to bring God's chosen people near to humanity and morals, to feel love to the Creator and their fellow creatures. This will explain the verse והיו הכרובים פורשי כנפים למעלה סוככים בכנפיהם על הכפרת ופניהם איש אל אחיו אל הכפרת יהיו פני הכרובים (שמות כ"ה ז') "And the Cherubim shall stretch forth their wings on high / covering the mercyseat with their wings and their faces shall look one to another, towards the mercyseat shall the faces of the Cherubim be" (Exod. XXV. 20.) The great Lawgiver meant thereby that the Cherubim, symbol of religion and creed shall spread their wings, shall turn their intentions heavenward to remind us about our likeness unto our heavenly Father. They shall further have the duty of guarding and watching over the mercyseat, the ten commandments, the place whence men gained light of life and joy and pleasure, whence came the shining sun or morality and humanity. Although all of us cannot agree in our ideas concerning the Supreme Being, yet all our ideas shall be turned one toward the other i. e., they shall not be opposed to one another, they shall aim at the same result, and as this can only be done if we all, like one man, strive to exercise true morals of humanity to do good and seek brotherhood, (therefore איש אל אחיו wordly translated "one towards his brother",) if we try to fulfil the Ten Commandments both with regard to God and to fellowman, then, ipso facto, they will turn their faces towards the mercyseat, towards the stone-tablets with the golden teachings of true religion, that holy treasure which alone leads to a happy and unclouded life.

In the next verse the two stonetablets are spoken of as עדות "testimony", two living and eternal witnesses. one pointing to our duties towards our Father in Heaven, the other reminding us of what we owe to our fellowmen. And the latter duties are innate with us i. e. we are taught them by a certain impulse of nature, so must the former be binding to us. And since we cannot behold our benevolent Father by means of our naked eye, we must arm ourselves with faith, with creed and faithfully believe in God's abundant love and mercy shown to us on every step in life.

Many of our ancient and modern philosophers cannot make belief agree with study, investigation and research. They ask: How may we investigate research, if we truly believe? And again, how can we faithfully believe, if we study and research? But the plain answer is: As men, gifted with sense and thought it is our duty to study and to investigate as far as our feeble human efforts can go, as far as our mind reaches. "Where understanding ends, there belief commences", where we can no more penetrate with our thought and reason, there we must, we are bound to believe. It is just absurd to belong to those light-minded men who believe in everything without previous investigation, and of whom our wise King Solomon said (משלי) פתי יאמין לכל דבר "A fool believeth in everything, as it is ridiculous and humilating to belong to those who believe nothing, who do not acknowledge the necessity of creed, who refuse to admit the fruit of an idea, though it leads them to good conclusions, and of whom the same wise King poet says: (שם) ובטח בלבו הוא כסיל "And he who confideth only in his own heart is an idiot".

We will always observe that every new idea, every new invention is always ridiculed and laughed at in the beginning by the greatest capacities of the day, and only after thorough examination, after due consideration of all its advantages it will be believed, it becomes admired, popular and a fact; the very same idea which years ago has been mocked by the most celebrated stars has established to its inventor an everlasting monument and an unforgotten memory. — Who for in-

instance believed Copernicus, when he so convicingly spoke of the revolving of the earth and stillstand of the sun? Who did not laugh at George Stephenson, when he undertook to produce the first railway engine? And yet have not both discoveries, on being thoroughly investigated and proved, gained the most laudable victory, have they not after due consideration was given them, done immense good, have they not opened an immense new field to the world at large, and do we not reward with a hearty laugh the incredulity of those, who, then stars of the day, did not believe the possiblity of this invention?

We will find the same with creed. We ought, nay, we must, we are bound to investigate, to search, to study everything we can with the help of our small human efforts, and where our understanding ends, there belief commences, what we cannot reach with our human sense that must be believed. But it is also certain, that the more we will understand the more will we yet find to believe! Now if in nature nothing is a fact, before it is subjected to a most minute investigation; if in our daily life, in studying the mysteries of nature, we are compelled to re-echo the words of Maimonides (רמב״ם) „תכלית הידיעה אשר נדע כי לא נדע״, "The aim of knowledge is to learn that we know nothing", how much more is this the case in supernatural subjects and ideas, where we grapple like blind men. We can easily compare this to one who, born blind, is anxious to distinguish one colour from the other. After all, we see that man possesses an innate sense of believing which is inseparable from our existence as reason and understanding. Those who feel an interest for Physiology and medicine will know how bodily abilities are connected with mental abilities, and this principle helps them to find out the reason of nervous diseases, paralysis etc.

The very learned Prof. Dr. Hufeland, late medical adviser to H. M. the King of Prussia has published a treatise on "Longevity", where he clearly explains how inseparable the bodily powers are from the mental abilities. This learned study has been read by the eminent philosopher Emanuel Kant, who fully agreeing with the views and conclusions of his colleague, published an explanatory essay entitled "on the power of the soul to master one's ill feelings by the strong will alone." The reference and relation between body and mind is being compared by Professor Hufeland to one riding on a wild horse, where, if he does not properly hold the reins and directs his horse, it will positively throw him down and wound him. So with our body and soul. The spirit of man is the rider, the body the animal, which must subdue to the rider's directions. If one can master his animal passions, he leads a happy and enviable life. Should the body not subdue but seek to master the soul then we see man hunting after all sorts of corruption and evil, and in the long run he looses his track and perishes amidst his passions. This comparison, concludes the learned philosopher, will tell the man the task of his life. Both Emanuel Kant and the Prof. Hufeland agree in the principle, that should man not allow his mind to be troubled with the feeling of illness, he would prevent disease entirely befalling him. Moreover, if he, when visited by illness, will not grieve about it, if he will not take it so very much to heart, but if he has courage enough to bear it bravely, not allowing sorrow to overpower him, he is sure to get sooner well than with the help of medicine. Besides, imagination plays a very important part in influencing the state of our body. We will often observe that an imaginary illness, i. e. that if it appeared to one that he is someway er other indisposed, this will weaken and discourage him so much, that it will in the long run cause real illness. On the other hand we can often see, that he who believes in mysterious powers and influences can easier be cured by such powers and influences than by medicine. The belief alone that a certain means will cure him, makes him cheerful and restores him ultimately to health. For instance: an illness caused by sudden grief can by remedied by sudden joy and vice versa. Generally speaking, the chief motive of illness of man is the interrupted action of his mental abilities on one hand — on the other. the growth of his bodily animal passions.

This idea in general, pronounced by Prof. Dr. Hufeland and confirmed by Emanuel Kant (1724—1804) was not new. It has been spoken of in the Thalmud in several places of which let us quote some. We find in Berachoth p. 60 (ברכות ס') משמועה רעה לא ירא נכון an explanation of the verse לבו בטוח בה' (תהלים קי״ב ז') "He is not afraid of evil tidings his heart is fixed trusting in God" (Psalms CXII, 7.) where each half of the verse is regarded to be an explanation to the other. The Thalmud tells us then of different Rabbis, who seeing their disciples in fear of something to come said to them, this fear will entail grief and sorrow, and after that illness and bodily harm.

We find in כל דקפיד קפיד בהדי (פסחים ק״י) "whoever is superstitious his superstition will become reality" (Pesachim 110). This was the state of "hypnotic suggestion" in the times gone by. But in course of centuries the study of hypnotism and nervous diseases has considerably advanced and improved, and we know now, how greatly our mental abilities are being influenced by our bodily power. Now-a-days, such a substance as p. e. pure water can on one hand make a healthy person ill — and on the other, the same water can restore health to a weak person. It is an open secret that just as nervous diseases can be and are being remedied by mysterious powers and imaginary influences, hypnotism can destroy many diseases, as long as and provided, that the original idea, the original imagination (Phantasie) of man has undergone some respective change or is done away with entirely. (It appears, curious as it may seem, that women, who were barren for years sometimes beget children, through outside influences, imagination or illusion of their being enceinte. There are some women, who, though childless for years, have begotten children, having been guided by the imagination, that a receipt of some Rabbi or otherwise pious and godfearing man has helped them to obtain their desire — a child. In one case a woman childless for 19 years was suddenly spoken of by one of her personal enemies, as being enceinte. Of course when this became known to her neighbours, they did so much molest her with questions about the truth of this statement, and her imagination grew so strong that, in the long run she was delivered of a child).

Having thus shown clearly, what power belief is able to exercise over mind of man, we arrive at the direct conclusion that the belief in a Supreme Being, which supervises, guides and directs our actions prevents us from comitting actions, which tend to disgrace us, cheers up our mind and renders us happy, satisfied and promotes our constant well being.

This conclusion has been also arrived at by the learned Rambam and is pronounced in his Moreh Nebuchim T. I. chap. 32, where he says that just as a healthy person who strains his eyes too much to see too small writing or for too great a distance becomes afterwards so weak-sighted, that he at last is unable to see a large type or a thing near him, and this is making him ill; so also if one overexerts his brains trying to deny facts, positive truth, for the denial of which he has no absolute foundation, he will in the long run become so disconfiding and wicked, that he will disbelieve or even attempt to deny such positive facts and events which really occured and are attested by eye-witnesses עיין מורה נבוכים ח' א' פ' ל"ב In this way he arrives at the verge of demoralisation and evildoing and entails the most harmful consequences to himself.

No wonder therefore, that as we will easily find after all that is said above, the socialists, those who teach social equality, equal distribution of labour and equal share in the good of life and living for all mankind, can do nothing good at present. They fight against a law of nature, a law, that is as eternal as the world, and in this attempt they become so weak-minded, so unreasonable, that they at last doubt facts, the truth of which is open to all. Now let us suppose for one moment that the world has attained that degree of perfection that labour is equally destributed and the profits equally shared between all human beings. It is well known that amongst all men we must find good workmen and artisans, i. e. such who attained the greatest perfection in their trade, medium workmen, i. e. such whose work though not the best, yet can satisfy the wants of the world, and unskilled workmen, i. e. such whose work is very far from good and leaves very much to be wished for. Also in food and necessaries of life we will find dear food which is rare and excellent, and cheap, ordinary food, of which we have always plenty at hand. Since there is always less of the good than of the ordinary, how shall we divide between all the articles made by skilled artisans or the dear and rare food, moreover since by natural impuls every human being wishes always to have the best he can find. If for instance it will be found practical to divide by casting lots, there will be some freethinkers who will say: "Why, we do not approve of lots for lots are a matter of luck, luck a matter of chance, chance a matter of belief, and since we are unbelievers, we cannot agree to lots, we want that all should be equal. Well, it seems on the other hand quite impossible to divide work among all without casting lots, so that all be satisfied. But as regards the good food, suppose we were to divide say twenty good and rare fishes between 6000 men, would we not then want to cast lots, deciding unto whose share shall fall the head parts and for whom should be the tail parts? And the freethinkers do not want any lots! There are also three classes of men according to their character, and as the good and perfect men have pleasure when they do good to somebody, so the bad men are pleased if they can wrong their fellowmen, even those who did them the greatest favours. They are ready to cause them the greatest trouble without pity or mercy. We find such not only amongst the uneducated classes, but even in high schools, in universities and in very influential positions in society. Some of these wicked individuals are very good and influential speakers and they have the power of attracting a great many, like magnetism. And such influence is constantly spreading like an epidemic or infectious disease and is being clad into refined modern names in order to dazzle the eyes of the hearers and make them think, that in following such ideas they do the best service to humanity. But this is only natural, and as long as the world will exist we will have such characters amongst us in hundreds, who, being treated most liberally by their fellow men, will always try to repay them with the greatest harm, will hate and despise each other. Just as we are told of Kain and Abel, who, though they were only two, and two brothers children of one father and brought up in one way, to share the whole world, yet hated and despised each other, and this hatred went so far that one — Cain — sought for means and found a way to remove his brother — Abel — from his way.

Just as we are told in the Torah to learn a moral from the history of Joseph and his brothers. Joseph saw many actions of his brothers which did not please him and without thinking anything bad he reported them, or as the Bible says, brought evil reports to his father. He did not do so of enmity nor did he wish to do them anything wrong, his desire was that their father should know and judge their actions. On the other hand Jacob as a good and loving father could only wish that Joseph should report to him all his (Jacob's) children did, for then he had a way to watch over their actions and to show them the way to do good. Yet, innocently as such informations were, were they not the reason of hatred and enmity between the brothers, hatred that went so far, that they were glad to find means to get rid of their brother. This shows us how difficult it is to maintain peace and concord in the midst of one family only. All the more difficult is it to keep a whole world together, to unite all mankind peacefully. For people always long for things they cannot reach, and as soon as they reach that they wished, there they want something else. There is no end to their achievments and no limit to their wants and wishes, as the Thalmud says מי שיש לו מנה רוצה מאתים "He who has one hundred coins wishes for two hundred" a. s. o. The more one has the more one wishes.

The so called anarchists desire that liberty and freedom should go sa far, that there should be no government at all, no rulers or kings. But this is quite impossible considering the so great difference existing between the character of one and another, as we have repeatedly shown.

I personally can have an idea how that free and happy land of the anarchists will be. In Russia which is only a half civilized country and its people are also not in a very high degree of civilisation, I have travelled through the greater part of the country without being interfered or molested in any way, but here in free and happy London—but how I must regret that freedom. My business compells me to go through a great many small streets and turnings, where I found a great many roughs congregated, who gamble and do other objectionable things. I have on many occasions narrowly escaped with my life by roughs throwing stones and other missiles at me, not counting the blows I have received and my clothes spoilt by the mud and other dirt thrown at me, and this has also happened to me in the open roads.

I greatly thank the nobility of England for their endeavours for making this the most enlightened country in the world, but the rough characters taking advantage of their position make it very hard and uncomfortable for the respectable person thus in England, where they have such a large body of police, such things are carried on, then how will I be in the happy land of the anarchists who wish to do away with the police entirely.

Well, it would be quite useless to address oneself to such socialists or anarchists, because they aim only at their own advantage and have only their own benefit at heart. They desire to become equal to the great bankers, to the wealthy men, who are blessed with a great fortune and plenty of means. For them words are purely wasted, because they are egotists, caring only for themselves. We wish only to speak to those, who really think of the benefit of the world at large, and who, by their brave actions proved that they wish to raise and really did raise the world to the present state of civilization. They must continue in their noble endeavours, but, so doing, not forget to consider well which of their ideas it is possible to realise, and which must remain only an illusion and can never become a fact. Then there are a great many cases where we must say with our Rabbis הלכה ואין מורין כן "though it is the law, yet we are not taught to do so". Just as with וזמרי Simri, who was put to death by Phinchas. According to jewish law it was not legal to slay him, but the Thalmud says קנאים פוגעין בו "Zeal of revenge overcame him".

As we have sufficiently proved, it is never possible to remove the evil entirely and to have the good. The רע the evil is, as we said, the twin-sister of the טוב the good, born at the same time and bred by one another. and we will never attain such a standard of perfect union as to free ourselves entirely from the bad and retain the good alone.

But should we for a moment suppose, that we have done away with all evil and retained the good, the perfect only, why, we will not feel, not know not recognise it, as we can have no idea of darkness, when constantly surrounded with light. After all it is the duty of man to try to improve the position of mankind, as far as it lies in our power, as we are commanded by our Torah to be liberal in the charity. In this case we might have possibly asked ourselves:— "Why should we give a man support, if it is not the will of the Almighty to let him have his wants in plenty? yet our law bids us that we must help the needy without asking why God does not grant him richess. Just so, although we may not be able to satisfy the whole human race, yet we must be merciful and try to think of a scheme, how we shall help those unfortunate men, who wish to work as good as they can or according to their good abilities and can find no employment. For there are many who would be only too glad to live most economically, were only occasion given to them to earn so much as to provide for their unconditional wants. We must, we are in duty bound to help such man, as it says in the Torah פתח תפתח את ידך לאחיך לעניך ולאביונך בארצך. (דברים ט״ו י״א) "Thou shalt open thy hand unto thy brother, the needy and to thy poor in thy land (Deut. XV, 11) and (שם) כי לא יחדל אביון "poverty will not cease" (ibid.) We must try and endeavour to help and support them, but the question arises, how? in which way? We can advise to establish a humane society in the strain described in this pamphlet. To enlist the sympathy of those who understand true and unbiassed religion to be founded only on the two chief principles "love of God and love of man" and that

— 84 —

all other principles in creed are but a way and means leading to these two great fundamental principles. We must not enter into investigation of the theory one or the other has formed of a Supreme Being, for as we explained above speaking of the Cherubim כרובים that it is impossible that all should have one thought, one idea, and that it is immaterial, however, one thinks as long as ופניהם איש אל אחיו all these ideas lead to and aim at one great principle "brotherhood". This society can join ministers of all creeds without distinction, though they are not bound to adhere all to the same minor principles. This society shall not make nationalism its chief point, but it shall be cosmopolitan. Nationalism is implanting only love to a certain nation working only in one direction, and as it is not necessary to have a society for teaching mothers to love their children, as this love is innate to human nature, so it is unnecessary to have a society for promoting nationalism, for it is a natural feeling that one must love his compatriots, but we must have a society to teach mothers to love strange children, and so must we have a society propagating cosmopolitism love to all human race.

This humane society shall establish a company on shares, which shall be at a moderate price, so that those who are not gifted with richess should also be able to purchase them and they shall buy plots of land and place at the disposal of the shareholders on terms of repayment by reasonable instalments with a small interest upon the capital part of which interest shall be used towards holding a ballot say twice a year. They shall also establish factories and workshops, where they will be able to give employment to those who are temporarily out of work and thus enable them to earn a respectable, if even not luxurious living, until they will have a better situation. This may also be done on shares, and from the profits thereof more land can be bought and more factories established every year. This society shall also endeavour to open free reading rooms and to find good speakers to propagate the ideas of humanity and also different branches of science. One of the duties of this society shall be to find cheap and comfortable dwellings for the poor so that a workingman will not be obliged, as it is now-a-days, to pay a considerable part of his earnings for a residence for himself and family. It will become the duty of these Societies to see at the same time to induce the working classes to lead a steady and modest life, that they may abstain from spending too much on drink, for the eight hours will then, and only then be a boon for the workingmen. To reach this it would seem advisable to suggest that about half an hour after the workingmen leave off work, all public beer and wine houses be closed. Very little good indeed can be expected to arise of an 8 hours work day if the free time left be spent in public houses. Let them rather, after they leave their work spend their time reading useful and instructive Books, hear good and educating lectures etc. Gambling is a vice and these societies will do a justice in influencing all their members, and we think it will be all the human race, to do away with it.

These Societies shall also try to pacify the Kings in a friendly way and thus to abolish all kinds of war and politica discord. Lastly every member of this society shall apply himself to study the universal language for all the world, either the Volapüc or the Esperand whichever the learned professors will decide upon. It is to be hoped that such societies can be established in a comparatively short time, and bring a great deal of good to all the world.

The next step, I would venture to propose, is to form a league between all the societies established all over Europe for humanitarian purposes, viz: all peace societies, the Anti-Anti-Semites in Germany, Austria etc.

When this is carried out with the help of God and His blessing, we hope to submit further schemes to promote the welfare and wellbeing of all our fellowmen.

Fortunately the English Press, both religious and political is free of ideas entailing the above mentioned deplorable consequences. The religious press will perhaps point out the better sides of that creed, for which it pleads, but it is liberal at the same time and will not attack any other creed, giving to each one due credit and respect. Just so the polical press pleading the cause of their party will manifest due esteem for the ideas of other parties. It is therefore that we must once more take the opportunity to express our gratitude to the English nobility, with His Eminence Cardinal Manning, the Lord Archbishop of London and Canterbury, the Lord Bishop of Ripon, the Earl of Meath, the Duke of Westminster etc. at the head, for the zealous endeavours, with which they make it their duty to remove the three mentioned obstacles to universal happiness.

It is the duty of all subjects of Her Most Gracious Britanic Majesty to implore the Almighty, to bless that country where the Ruler is merciful, kind and humane, the clergy benevolent, peace-seeking and peace-loving and the press furthering the interests of all shades and !classes of the population.

18). We have here to deal with 2 questions: 1) the Colonisation of Palestine, 2) Agriculture as a means of livelihood. Concerning the Colonisation of Palestine, we will find some of our Rabbis, if we guide ourselves by the Thalmud, who were expressly and distincly against it. — Our Sages say: אמר ר' יהודה כל העולה מבבל לארץ ישראל עבר בעשה שנאמר בבלה (ירמיהו) יבאו ושמה יהיו עד יום פקדי אתכם נאום ה' "Rabbi Jehudah says: Whosoever goes from Babylon to Palestine, transgresses a commandment, for it is said in Jeremiah: To Babylon shall ye come and there shall ye stay until the day when I will visit you, saith the Lord. (Kessuboth 111.) Rabbi Zeira, who was very much devoted to the Holy Land did not fall in with the views of Rabbi Jehudah, who, wishing to go to Palestine had to keep such desire secret. Yet he acknowledges the three oaths above referred to and says that by going to and settling in the Holy Land, wd need not we dare not anticipate the Almighty with any plans whatsoever regarding the Millennium, who many times showed plainly his great love to the Holy Land, and who is the author of many highly sympathetic remarks on the subject, says after all, when speaking of the three oaths: אם אתם מקימים טוב ואם לאו אני מתיר את בשרכם כצבאות וכאילות השדה "If you obey, well and good. — if not I will make your lives as that of the gazelle and of the hart". Rabbi Eliezer with his farsightedness understood that there will be a time when agriculture will be the principal means of livelihood. This is expressed in Rabbi Eliezer's words עתירין כל בעלי האמניות שיעמדו על הקרקע שנאמר וירדו מאניותיהם כל תפשי משוט מלחים כל חובלי הים על הארץ "There will be a time when all tradesmen will become יעמדו workers on the soil as it says in Ezechiel: All that handle the oar, the mariners and all the pilots of the sea shall come down from the ships, they shall stand upon the land". (Jebamoth 63). But, he says further, the expression ירדו "they went down" shows, that the world will not make a progress but a regress, a step not up but down, שאין לך אומנת פחותה מן הקרקע "For there is no trade inferior to agriculture. We read about him in the same tractat, that when he once met an agricultural labourer at work he told him הפיכא בעסקא טוב מינך "He who circulates his money in business does better than you".

We find also in the Thalmud that Rav expressed himself in the same manner seeing once as the ears of corn lifted up their heads proudly waving in the air (ibid.) Rovo says: מאה זוזי בעסקא בשרא וחמרא — בארעה מלחה והפירה ולא עוד אלא מגני לו ארעה ומרמי לו תגרא "A hundred florins in business enable a man to have daily meat and wine, a hundred florins in soil, only bread and salt and moreover make a man sleep on the floor and entail aggrivation." (Jebamoth 63). Therefore we can learn, that although we may love Palestine as devoutedly as Rabbi Zeira and Rabbi Eliezer and Rovo yet we may do so only, because Palestine remains to us a living eternal memorial of our great historic past, but we must never allow ourselves to think of other different reasons. Concerning agriculture as the principal means of livelihood and the absolute necessity of mankind to invest capital in ground, we hear different opinions of our Rabbis. Though Rabbi Eliezer, as we have seen above, does not think agriculture profitable, yet he says: כל מי שאין לו קרקע אינו אדם דכתיב השמים שמים לה' והארץ נתן לבני אדם "Whoever has no soil is not a man for it says: The heavens are for God and the earth he gave unto sons of man" (Psalms CXV. 16). He certainly wishes every man to know that it is good to buy soil for his money, but at the same time he concurs with the advice of another Rabbi לעולם ישליש אדם מעותיו שליש "A man shall בקרקע שליש במו"מ ויתן שליש תחת ידו (ב"מ מ"ב) divide his money into three parts, investing one third in ground, one third putting into business and keeping a third in cash in hand". Thus a man can always be provided for. What he does not earn of his soil he replenishes from his business and if both fail to make up sufficient for his living, the cash in hand balances the account. If we would thus like to think of a scheme for the colonisation of Palestine, we should understand, that every one should invest only a certain part of his financial means in soil in Palestine, and for this purpose there is only one practical way to establish a Company on shares giving every one the privilege of having as many shares as he likes, and making their prices so moderate, as to give everyone, rich and poor alike, access to them. To arrive at this end by means of small contributions, donations and charity, is by all means a failure.

Our Sages have expressed this very theory in the following words: גדולה גמילות חסד יותר מן הצדקה "Acts of kindness by way of business are preferable to charity". They base this theory on the verse זרעו לכם לצדקה וקצרו לפי חסד and put (צדקה) charity on a levell with sowing, while חסד businesslike acts of kindness is to them on a levell with harvest, because charity is as doubtful in its results like the seed one throws on the field without any guarantee of its taking root and yelding a good harvest whilst חסד is something substantial like the harvest.

Considering that Palestine cannot hold all Jews in existence, and further how beneficial it is for the world at large that Jews are dispersed throughout all parts, as we find in Pesachim ע"א בין שפורם לישראל הקב"ה עשה צדקה "The Allmighty has shown His love to Israel in spreading them all over the habitable globe", we would think that not only must we not be against, but it is our duty to encourage all facilities offered by the generous Baron de Hirsch and others who wish to transplant and colonise our brethren in other parts of the world besides Palestine, leaving at the same time to those who prefer the Holy Land opportunity to dwell there.

Speaking on this subject we may add that the meaning of the Rabbis is that, while Israel is spread all over the globe, people notice them less and are usually left alone, while where they congregate in a particular spot, they are unwillingly calling upon them the attention of their surroundings which is not always favourably disposed towards them, and should the Jews settle *en masse* in Palestine they would immediately awake the envy of their enemies and who knows if the Sultan's successors will be so very anxious to protect them.

19.)—Commenting on Isiah LVIII, 14, והאכלתיך נחלת יעקב אביך "And I shall feed thee with the heritage of Jacob thy father". The Middrash asks why expressly of Jacob? and answers: because unto him God said: ופרצת ימה וקדמה צפונה ונגבה (בראשית כ"ח י"ו) "And thou shalt spread abroad to the west, and to the east and to the north and to the south" which means that the idea of knowledge of God and love to our fellowmen will spread all over the habitable globe.

According to the theory which I endeavour to explain throughout this work, it is clearly seen, that all our holy law is founded only on love of man and love to a stranger especially which, eo ipso, teaches us and shows us the way how we can love our Creator and cleave unto him.

Following this theory we will now understand the meaning of the verse ומכה אדם יומת "Whosoever killeth a man shall die (Levit. XXIV, 21.) The late Rev. Dr. N. M. Adler in his famous commentary to the Bible asks, why the Thargum translates ומכה by וקטלינא (kill) in opposition to all other commentaries, who say that ומכה. means "bruise, smite, wound" and אדם refers to "a father"? The comentators base their opinion on the fact that, since in v. 17 of the same chapter it says ואיש כי יכה כל נפש אדם מות יומת "And a man who slayeth any human being shall surely be put to death", it would be needless to repeat a commandment a few verses later, which would convey quite the same meaning. But guided by the rules which precede those notes, we find here v. 17 dealing with two quite different subjects which are subsequently explained collectively. On this principle the repetition is easily explained.

When Moses has comanded his peoble ואיש כי יכה כל נפש אדם מות יומת (v. 17. אדם meaning Jews only as explained), he was affraid that his hearers will not include also every other human being, therefore he was compelled afterwards to repeat (v. 21) ומכה אדם יומת continuing in v. 22 משפט אחד יהיה לכם כגר כאזרח יהיה "Ye shall have one manner of law as well for the stranger as for the citizen of your own country" and concluding as usually אני ה' with the intention of pointing to God as the ideal of the best qualities, whom men must endeavour to resemble.

We will also understand the meaning of Mendelsohn

who in the verse לנכרי תשיך translates נכרי not stranger (of another creed) but a "foreigner". In Levit. XXV, 35, we read: "And if וכי ימוך אחיך ומטה ידו עמך והחזקת בו גר ותושב וחי עמך thy brother be waxen poor and fallen in decay with thee, then thou shalt relieve him a stranger or a sojourner that he may live with thee". Hereafter follow verse 36 and 37 the former dealing about charging one interest on money lent to him and concluding again with וחי אחיך עמך "and thy brother shall live with thee" and the latter about paying interest on monies lent to us and concluding with אני ה' אלהיכם in v. 39. One of these verses would seem superfluous as since we are once told not to charge interest, it is evident that we should not give our monies away for interest. But the great legislator acted here according to rule 2 of these three rules preceeding these notes i. e. he first included two subjects into one verse and then explained them in particular. Thus for אחיך he says: (v. 36) אל תקח מאחיך נשך ותרבית וכו' וחי אחיך עמך "Thou shalt not take from him usury or increase etc. and *thy brother* shall live with thee". For the stranger, sojourner or foreigner he says in v. 37 את כספך לו תתן לו בנשך "Thy money shalt thou not give him for usury" and concluding as usual with אני ה'. We are thus equally forbidden to take any interest from our debtors as to pay any interest on the loan to our creditors. And naturally since Palestine has never been a manufacturing country, and agriculture was the principal means of livelihood, it could not pay an agriculturer to borrow money on interest, not only to or from Jews but from all even strangers dwelling in our land.

Moses has also seen that, if Jews would even like to lend out money without interest, they could by no means lend it out to all who would want it. Therefore he had to make a distinction between the citizen and sojourner in in our land, and the foreigner dwelling in a neighbouring country, and being only in commercial connection with us. This will now throw full light upon the above brought verse in Deut. where נכרי means a foreigner, living outside our land and being connected with us only in business. That only a foreigner and not a non Jew living in our country has been meant by Moses, will be clearly visible if we read the contumation of v. 35 in Levit XXV. גר ותושב וחי עמך A stranger (non Jew living in our country) or sojourner and he shall live with thee, i.e. that any men Jew or non-Jew living in our land has to enjoy the same equal rights and must be supported. But, we may charge interest on monies we lend out to foreigners i.e. people living in other neighbouring countries, otherwise, we would as above explained not be able to do any business. It is peculiar that תשיך is put in the מפעיל (transitive) meaning originally: pay interest. We may thus explain the verse also so, that not only may we take interest from, but we are to pay interest to the foreigner, when lending money to him or borrowing some from him as the case may be.

A proof that נכרי means only a non-jewish foreigner is to be seen in the fact, that every law given for the נכרי is immediately followed by another for אחיך meaning that all Jews even those dwelling in foreign lands, owing to their small number and relationship, had to equally enjoy the prilvileges and bear the hardships of the law, whilst a non-jewish foreigner was subject to a different law, which in some cases was more beneficial to him in his daily life.

This would justify Rabenu Saadia Gaon רבינו סעדיה הגאון

who quotes לנכרי תשיך amongst the 248 commandments מצות עשה of the Holy Writ, i. e. If a non-jewish foreigner is promised interest on money he lends to us, we must pay him, whilst if we even promise interest to any Jew we need not pay it to him (as according to the Talmud). At the same we will find right what the Rambam רמב"ם ז"ל says that we are allowed to charge interest to any non-jewish foreigners on monies we lend them, quoting the words of the Mishna לוין ומלוין להם "we may borrow from and lend to them" first specifying לוין — the borrowing — and contending that just as we may pay a non-jewish foreigner interest for money he lends us, we may, eo ipso, charge interest on monies borrowed from us, otherwise we should always be at a loss.

That strangers-non-Jews residing in our country must be treated like our own brethren is also proved by Deutr. XV 2, 3, where it says: לא יגש את רעהו ואת אחיו וכו' את הנכרי תגיש "He shall not exact it from his friend nor of his brother etc. thou mayest exact it of the foreigner". Here רעהו means the non-jewish citizen and אחיו his Jewish brethren, otherwise it would not be distinctly placed in two expressions n t related to each other. Moses wished us to understand that all our citizen jews or non-jews who dwell with us, must equally enjoy the privilege of the שמטה — year of release — whilst the foreigner can have no right to its benefits. Just so he wished us to understand that by lending out money to our citizens without interest, to foreigners on interest and so borrowing money from each, we will be able to support one another in time of need as he says, referring to both רבית ושמטה interest and year of release: אפס כי לא יהיה בך אביון "in order that there shall be no poor amongst you" (Deut.

XV. 4.) That all poor must be dealt with mercifully without distinction of nationality as long as they live with us is also seen of verse 11 in the same chapter כי לא יחדל אביון מקרב הארץ על כן אנכי מצוך לאמר פתח תפתח את ידך לאחיך לעניך ולאביונך בארצך (שם י"א) "For the poor will never cease within the land therefore I command thee thou shalt surely open thy hand to *thy brother, thy poor* and *thy needy* in thy land [thy brother Jews, thy poor and thy needy — non-jewish strangers].

A similar instance can be given from Levit. XIX, 12, לא תעשוק את רעך "Thou shalt not opress thy friend" and Deutr. XXIV, 14, לא תשיך שכיר עני ואביון מאחיך או מגרך אשר בארצך בשעריך "Thou shalt not oppress an hired servant that is poor and needy whether he be of thy brethren or thy strangers that are in thy land within thy gates". In the word עמיתך the expressions גר ותושב are included, therefore we find them placed one instead of the other to show that all are placed under the same law. (see Levit XIX, 11, 19 where we find עמיתך (thy neighbour) רעך (thy friend) אחיך (thy brother) subject to the same law and placed one beside and also instead of the other.

But if slavery was really so great a hardship, how could Moses, the great and human legislator have allowed Jews to keep slaves? This question which is very important to all who study the Bible, can also be easily answered following this theory. I have tried to point out several times that Moses was compelled to give his people some laws, which were only suited for the time, they were given at. He went so far as to allow his followers to listen unto another prophet after his death and to do what he biddeth, although it may perhaps be not in accordance with or commenting the law of Moses. Now if we follow up history, we will find that when Moses gave these laws they were absolutely indispensable. At that time slaves were held by all nations, and those slaves were brutally illtreated, depending with their life and death, on their breadgivers. Moses' laws had to warn the people of Israel from doing so. On the contrary Moses wished to take off the burden entirely from the non-jewish slave's shoulders who was employed by an Israelite. Every servant, argued Moses, be he whoever he is, must be politely dealt with. We find him still further advanced, if we look into Deut. XXIII, 16-17, לא תסגיר עבד אל אדוניו אשר ינצל אליך מעם אדוניו עמך ישב בקרבך במקום אשר יבחר באחד שעריך וכו' "Thou shalt not deliver unto his master a servant that is escaped from his master unto thee. He shall dwell with thee even among you in that place which he will choose in one of thy gates, where it liketh him best, thou shalt not oppress him. (This law is still now acted upon in several civilized countries). He prohibited his people to buy slaves and keep them for ever. If they took a hebrew servant he was to serve a term of 6 years and on the seventh he was set free with gifts and presents according to the richess of his master. During the whole time of service such servant had to be treated in the kindliest way. Just so a non-jewish servant had to be dealt with in the most civil manner. Every wrong done to him personally, every bodily harm caused to him, entailed his full liberty, as we find in Exodus XXI, 26, 27 וכי יכה איש את עין עבדו או את עין אמתו להפשי ישלחנו תחת עינו וכו' "And if a man smite the eye of his servant or the eye of his maid that it perish, he shall let him go free for his eye's sake etc. All servants male or female, Jews and non-jews had to rest on Sabbath, had not to be oppressed etc." Such and other rights and privileges made the service not a burden but a pleasant duty, and no wonder that a great many of the non-jewish slaves oppressed by non-jewish masters envied the servants of the Jews and wished to become subordinates to an Isralite. Thus it came that, when such slaves who succeeded to escape from their master's house were well cared for, those who were less fortunate in trying to gain their personal freedom, were bought by Jews for money. Were the Jews not to buy these slaves, they would have lead a very sad course of life as they were entirely, their life and death, freedom and person, in the hands of their masters.

But again the Jews could not buy away all slaves, as their number was large and whilst it wanted a vast amount of money and would make those who spend much for this purpose poor, what had, as above said, to be avoided. Thus the jews took as many slaves as they chose for their own use, to attend to their personal wants, and very soon both the master as well as the servant greatly profited. For while the master was replaced in instances of hard work by a trustworthy and faithful servant the servant was kindly treated and had ample opportunity to learn off the jews the morals of religion, principles of morality, and humanity. One hand washed the other. The beneficial influence of mutual support we can even observe now-a-days between England and the far parts of India, Africa and Australia. Whilst the latter is taught by scientific Englishmen principles of humanity, modesty, religion and knowledge, the former derives the great material benefit of their produce. Although I have shown myself to be a great antagonist of wars for political reasons, I must say that to lead an army against a land and to conquer it with the view of propagating there humanity and morals of religion is not only right but it is even the duty of the more civilized nations.

In consideration of all that has been said in this pamphlet, we will now see that. the verse which I have placed in the commencement of this essay, will also explain the two following verses, treating about honesty in weights and measure. Many students of the Bible are surprised why these verses terminate with אני ה׳ "I am the Lord". In Levit. XIX, 33. the passage commences with וכי יגור אתכם גר בארצכם לא תונו אתו "And if a stranger sojourn with thee in your land ye shall not oppress him Then comes the verse 33 given in full on p. 1., which is then. followed by v. 34 an explanation of the foregoing verses, to show where we must take care to be honest with and not to cheat a stranger, dwelling with us, that we must have full and just weights, scales and measures, that we must exercise justice and be straightforward, and concluding as usually when referring to love towards strangers with אני ה׳ to point to the ideal of all perfection as to an example for mankind.

We find in Tractat (חולין צ״ד) אסור לגנוב דעת הבריות אפילו עכו״ם "It is forbidden to defraud the opinion of people, even of non jews i. e. that we must not act so as to give anyone reason to have an incorrect opinion about us.

In Tractat עבודה זרה ג׳ we read עכו״ם עוסק בתורה הרי הוא ככהן גדול דכתיב אשר יעשה אותם האדם וחי בהם "A non-jew studying the law is equal to a high priest for it says, that *the man* shall do them and live thereby".

I beg to convey my humble and most heartfelt thanks to his Majesty the Sultan of Turkey for his human treatment towards his Jewish subjects, and I also wish to convey my grateful thanks to Baron Edmond de Rothschild in spending such vast sums of money, not in stone monuments but in living monuments, and I also wish to gratefully thank the Rothschilds for their sterling friendship and trueheartedness towards their co-religionists. But above all I wish my humble and grateful thanks to be conveyed to Baron de Hirsch. Since the world exists there has not been such another, who has spent so many millions and who intends giving many millions more, for the better welfare and to place in a better condition millions of his humble persecuted co-religionists and I am greatly pleased that Baron de Hirsch has all the same ideas as I have, and also by planting the Jews in different parts, it will not alone be good for the Jews but for the Christians as well, for the Jews are like spice, a little of it gives great flavour to the food, put too much of it in the food and the result is the food is spoilt thus showing that if the Jews are settled in different parts of the world they will show a good example to their christian neighbours by their energy and thrift, and it is a great deal better that the Jews should have a voice in different parliaments of the world than to live in one place like China and to have a consul, but we can see by facts that the Americans do not greatly respect the Chinese who have a consul as much as the Jews who have no consul.

○ ○ ○

Just a short remark on the charity exercised by the local Board of Guardians:—

It has been repeatedly proved in this essay that the good and the evil are two sisters, twins; born at the same time and created by the cause, and the more we try to ameliorate something, the more place will still remain for new improvements, new corrections.

We admit the importance of charity and it is just for this reason that we crave permission of the generous donors who are constantly devoting their abundant means for this noble purpose to submit to them the important points about it and about the way it is now given. Though it is and remains a fact that, however we may try, we will never get rid of such impostors, who whilst they make us believe by means of false statements that they are destitute and poor, are in fact not in want of our support and charity, yet we cannot say that because of these impostors we should not support and help the really deserving poor? The Thalmud, speaking of impostors above allued to, says: באו ונחזיק טובה לרמאים "let us be thankful to the cheats". And we must really thank them, for how could we otherwise face the question: Why are so many poor left without assistance? As it is we can and do reply: Why, there are so many impostors, that one cannot distinguish the deserving case from the fraud and therefore we refuse so many.

We would like to see the charity so dealt with, that at least the really deserving man be not worse off than the impostor. Hitherto we met a great many really deserving and pressing cases unattended to or refused, because the applicants cannot or will not humble themselves too much, or, as the impostors usually do, take recourse to false statements, in order to satisfy the requirements of the rules. Should there, however, happen an exceptional case where a honest man has been driven by want and misery to state an untrue fact, it is at once found out, it is seen in his face, and as a punishment naturally follows—a refusal point blank. It is our duty to remedy and prevent such unpleasant and heartrending occurrences, and for this purpose it is most advisable to arrange that the distribution of charity should not be through certain individuals especially appointed for the purpose. They in their constant rounds to the poorest of the poor become so used to the cry of hunger, need and starvation, that special important cases never influence them. They hear mechanically, reply and act instinctively; crying, sobbing, tears are constant details of their daily round and must, by sheer force of habit, discontinue to impress them.

We venture to suggest the following remedy. Every one desirous of being helped or supported by or through the Board of Guardians should find an introduction or recommendation from the President or Vice President of any society, Synagogue (in which case also from the acting minister) or public body of which he is a member. Should it happen that the applicant is not on the list of any of these establishments, he is sure to find friends, countrymen or acquaintances who will take the trouble to get such an introduction for him. In that introduction, which of course, must be given only after a thorough investigation of the case and must contain a true and unbiassed statement, can be mentioned the applicant's past position, his abilities, or other reasons why he may be specially recommended. Such application being laid before the Board, they may, if they think fit re-investigate the case before they decide upon.

Such introduction need not be handed over by the applicant personally. It may be forwarded to the Board by

Post, as may also the respective amounts voted by the Board in every case. This would do away with the overcrowding of the doors of the Board's offices by *many* daily, a circumstance which causes illfeeling towards us from our gentile neighbours. It is most important, that the ministers of congregations should not refuse a recommendation to a man they know as deserving. Treated thus, the deserving man, who usually humbly begs for support, will not be worse off than the impostor who boldly compels to assist him, and the help so given will be granted in a really humane manner.

If this practical scheme is adopted it would be most advisable to reduce the amount of money distributed as charity, and in its stead to increase the amount lent out as loans, making them repayable by small instalments, ad minimo, and at intervals best convenient to the position of the borrower. As it is now greater difficulties are experienced when applying for a loan, than when asking for charity. Yet we are taught by our sages גדול גמילות חסדים יותר מן הצדקה "the loan money (acts of kindness) is greater than the giving of charity". And indeed by giving alms we make a man a professional beggar, and so reduce him to the state of self negligence, humiliation and beggary, whilst a loan, by virtue of its being repaid, induces and encourages a man to work. We have often seen that one who is used to receive charity, will always want and need it, nay he will get lazy to work and depend on it, whilst a honest man who being poor cannot for one or another reason get a loan, will always blush with shame, thinking he had to accept charity from the Board. Charity should only be given to sick and disabled persons. They are fully entitled to claim it by virtue of their being unable to work.

But if he is granted a loan, let it be given to repay in such instalments the borrower is able to stand and let him be allowed to repay it at any time he will be able according to his circumstances. It would be advisable that the Board should charge interest say one shilling in the Pound. This will on one hand not make any difference to the borrower on the other it will considerably increase the income of the Board.

The Board should also do away with demanding from the borrower securities when applied to for a loan. For being on friendly terms with somebody and not being able to refuse doing him so great a favour as signing a loan as surety, why should a person so signed have to suffer, if the borrower is temporarily unable to pay his instalments? Especially if the Board by lending this money means to exercise charity. If the borrower can not repay the instalments of his loan due in a time given to him, and the Board consequently takes steps to recover this debt from the surety, who had no benefit of it whatsoever, in order to do with the money so received other charity, would that charity than not be a מצוה הבאה בעבירה "a virtue done by means of vice"? We know many who were reduced to utter poverty and destitution, nay, they had even to leave the country, house, home and family, solely because they meant to help some of their friends in becoming sureties for them. According to the present arrangements it is so, that when one of the applicants for a loan is sent before the Committee of the Board, they ask him:— "Have you no friends at all"?— It is only natural that he cannot reply in that case that those friends he has are already burdened as sureties at private Loan Offices, and that, coming to the Board of Guardians, he has no other place where his application should be granted, and that the Board is his last means of salvation! Most of the honest and respectable poor would rather, if they could, go somewhere else and pay interest than stand for hours and await their turn before the officers of the Board in a crowd of so mixed a character as we may see there daily. The Board on their part could only secure themselves so much that they make it a duty of those who introduce the applicants to them, to keep a watching eye over the state of affairs of the borrower, and to use their best influence with him should it happen that he can pay and would not, and to report change of residence etc. It is to be hoped that the losses, which may arise from this way of conducting the business of the Board will not be as great at they may at first sight appear. Why, do we not see a great many shops and travellers giving away their goods on weekly payments and making a first class living, even accumulating a considerable profit, though they are likely to have a great risk. The interest of one shilling in the pound proposed to be charged by the Board might also cover the expenses of keeping a paid collector to call upon the borrowers and get from them the small instalments such borrowers do pay, as practice shows that when a collector calls, he easily gets a small amount whilst one cannot always find time to go to the offices of the Board with a small account, nor is it sometimes worth the trouble. It is impossible morover, when the husbands are out at work and the wives have little children to look after and nobody to leave at home.

The rules of the Board should be so framed that they be especially lenient to such applicants, who are introduced to the Board on special recommendation either for their past position, carreer, piety, learning etc. It is so in other countries where people recommended on this basis are especially cared for, that they live respectably by the support of their co-religionists, whilst here one can often find them in a deplorable condition.

One more point remains to touch upon. If the Board considers and decides cases, when the applicants are to be sent away to their native or another country, let them not delay the execution of their decision so long. As it is, one, who after a struggle and long weeks' waiting, at last gets the fare home or elsewhere has to wait weeks and weeks during which time his board and lodging cost him as much as he may well pay for the fare, and so it is that יצא שכרו בהפסידו his gain is devoured by his loss. Now what if, as in most cases it really is, the applicant has only limited means or none at all, and cannot stand the expense of keeping body and soul together during the long interval between the decision of the Board and its execution? He then of course undergoes a long list of privations and suffering, waiting for his help to come. Would that this be avoided and the assistance rendered by the Board will be humane and beneficial to the needy, a pride and an honour to the community and a good example to others.

And it would also be of inestimable good if there would be an employment bureau, where workmen out of employment could apply for work, and that employers requiring men should also apply to the bureau, but I wish to state that two persons should be appointed whose duty it should be to look for situations for those out of work. It would greatly relieve the Board of large sums that they give in charity for temporary relief, whilst by finding employment for those out of work, they would do permanent good.

APPENDIX.

The following few words will explain some expressions which might, as they are, be misunderstood or misinterpreted:—

Page 1, Line 1. אשרי הדור שהגדולים נשמעים לקטנים (ריה כ"ה)
Page 6, Line 27. אין אליהו בא לטמא תטהר רק לרחק המקורבים בזרוע ולקרב המורחקים בזרוע (סוף עדיות).

Page 5, line 9, page 14, line 4, page 43, line 5. The passages here quoted distinctly prove the importance of cosmopolitism.

Page 8, line 7. See Gen. III. 5, והייתם כאלהים יודעי טוב ורע

Page 18, line 5. הדן דין אמת לאמתו Here the word לאמתו seems superfluous, for if a judge gives "right judgment" it is certainly given in its perfect truth. But it is possible that conforming with the letter of the law, a Judge can sometimes sentence a man to a punishment which he does not deserve in this case. It is therefore incumbent upon a judge to investigate a case thoroughly not being guided by the letter of the law alone. He must even sometimes act above his authority לפנים משורת הדין as we find in the Thalmud לא חרבה ירושלים אלא מפני שהעמידו דיניהם על דין תורה (ב"מ ל') "Jerusalem has not been destroyed but because they have given judgment according to the letter of the law (Baba Meziah 30). We can learn therefrom that the distributors of charity ought to consider the circumstances of the cases more than the rules.

Page 55, line 17. אמת means manners.

Page 63, line 23. The passage from the Moreh Nebochim here quoted refers to the end of the previous page (62).

Page 73, line 22. See Ecclesiastes VII, 15-18.

Page 87, line 8. אין אדם מת וחצי תאותו בידו A man dies not possessing the half of what he desires.

Page 90, line 19 Because Palestine is considered holy by many nations on the habitable globe.

Page 94, line 5. This passage of the Rambam is not rightly understood

Page 95, line 14 and page 98 line 18. See Baba Meziah 59. (ב"מ נ"ט).

Page 96, line 28. The same refers to one knocking out his servants tooth as in next verse.

Page 97, line 12. Between "slaves" and "as" the words "and set them free" should be inserted.

ERRATA.

Page			*instead*	Movemements	*read*	Movements
,,	V	line 4			,,	world because these
,,	V	,, 5			,,	pleasure every class
,,	V	,, 17			,,	But the same
,.	VIII		,,	amngst	,,	amongst

PAGE	LINE	INSTEAD	READ	PAGE	LINE	INSTEAD	READ
1	3	24	34	23	24	Rusia	Russia
5	9	land	earth	25	20	gramble	grumble
6	20	af	of	28	19	ond	and
6	23	LIX	XLIX	28	26	rigth	right
6	30	oats	oaths	31	20	as	so
7	4	oats	oaths	31	30	Hisp eople	His people
7	17	"two"	to be omitted	33	26	six	five
7	19	his	His	34	17	simult-	simult-
8	19	"when"	to be omitted			anously	aneously
9	28	ect.	etc.	36	7	לבביך	לבבך
10	12	human	humane	36	22	כסוסד	כסותך
11	10	ours	our	37	4	chose	choose
11	21	peacefull	peaceful	38	3	whealthy	wealthy
13	3	human	humane	39	27	poeple	people
14	22	human	humane	40	17	suould	should
14	23	fo	to	41	1	ot	of
15	14	despisable	despicable	44	28	daggling	dazzling
15	24	boast	boasts	45	21	human	humane
16	2	prices	prizes	46	17	course	curse
16	5	aught	ought	47	27	onother	another
18	15	advice	advise	48	18	XYXI	XXXI
18	30	human	humane	48	21	refereed	referred
19	20	is—has	are—has	48	26	thousanth	thousand
19	29	costumer	customer	49	1	memorate	commemorate
20	2	creat	create	51	25	things	evil
20	30	ful	full	52	10	consevie	conceive
23	6	Governement	Government	53	7	whilst	while

PAGE	LINE	INSTEAD	READ	PAGE	LINE	INSTEAD	READ
54	15	desease	disease	86	15	polical	political
55	8	found	founded	87	16	wd	we
56	28	creat	create	87	21	טוב	כיטב
57	25	accout	account	89	22	חסד	חסדים
60	2	undertakes	undertake	89	26	levell	level
60	11	theym ay	they may	89	29	yeluing	yielding
62	11	subject	subjects	91	20	peoble	people
62	20	יורע	יודעי	92	17	מאחיך	מאתו
63	5	hoth	both	92	20	לו	לא
63	15	wifes	wives	93	2	in	to be omitted
63	18	irom	from	93	12	men	man
64	8	החים	החיים	93	26	prilvileges	privileges
67	22	full with	full of	94	16	תניש	תנוש
68	2	materiai	material	95	4	ידך	ידך
70	5	eat	ate	95	11	תשיך	תעשק
70	17	hat	that	95	22	human	humane
71	10	o	of	98	28	human	humane
72	28	the	as the	98	30	in	for
73	19	fruit	fact	100	15	allued	alluded
76	4	er	or	102	20	money	of money
79	8	impuls	impulse	104	8	officers	offices
81	10	sa	so	104	30	morover	Moreover
82	10	them	there				

www.ingramcontent.com/pod-product-compliance
Lightning Source LLC
Chambersburg PA
CBHW020137170426
43199CB00010B/778